arnold's fitness for kids

ages birth–5

doubleday

new york

london

toronto

sydney

auckland

arnold's fitness for kids

ages birth–5
a guide to health,
exercise, and nutrition

arnold schwarzenegger
with charles gaines

illustrations by jackie aher and denise donnell

Finished art assisted by Douglas Reinke

published by doubleday

a division of Bantam Doubleday Dell Publishing Group, Inc.
666 Fifth Avenue, New York, New York 10103

doubleday and the portrayal of an anchor with a
dolphin are trademarks of Doubleday, a division of
Bantam Doubleday Dell Publishing Group, Inc.

Book design by Marysarah Quinn and Claire N. Vaccaro
Hand lettering and endpapers by Robert deMichiell

Library of Congress Cataloging-in-Publication Data
Schwarzenegger, Arnold.
　[Fitness for kids ages birth–5]
　Arnold's fitness for kids ages birth–5 : a guide to health, exercise, and
nutrition / Arnold Schwarzenegger with Charles Gaines.—1st ed.
　　p.　cm.
　Includes bibliographical references.
　Summary: Discusses fitness, nutrition, and exercise and suggests
exercises and other activities suitable for young children.
　1. Bodybuilding for children—Juvenile literature.　2. Exercise for
children—Juvenile literature.　3. Children—Nutrition—Juvenile
literature.　[1. Physical fitness.　2. Exercise.　3. Nutrition.]
I. Gaines, Charles, 1942–　.　II. Title.　III. Title: Fitness for kids
ages birth–5.
GV546.6.C45S36　1993
646.7′5—dc20　　　　　　　　　　　　92-26209
　　　　　　　　　　　　　　　　　　CIP
　　　　　　　　　　　　　　　　　　AC

ISBN 0-385-42266-0

To my wife Maria
and our daughters
Katherine and Christina.
—Arnold Schwarzenegger

This series is also dedicated
to the world's children with
the wish that we could give
every one of them the
priceless gift of lifelong
fitness and good health.
—Arnold Schwarzenegger
and Charles Gaines

contents

introduction: A Note to Parents from Arnold   **1**

chapter 1: What You Can Do to Prepare Your Infant, Toddler, and Preschooler for Lifetime Fitness   **13**

chapter 2: Smart Nutrition for Your Infant, Toddler, and Preschooler   **47**

chapter 3: Outside the Home   **61**

appendix: Play Exercises for Kids from Birth Through Age Five   **79**
    part i: Birth to One Year   **81**
    part ii: One Year to Three Years   **89**
    part iii: Three Years to Six Years   **93**

bibliography   **104**

acknowledgments   **106**

iNTRoDUCTiON

a note to parents from arnold

I have always believed in getting things done—in meeting challenges head-on and solving problems before they get out of hand. To my mind, the single most serious and challenging fitness problem facing America today is the steady decline in the physical fitness of our children. There are plenty of statistics out there to back me up:

▶ Recent studies on millions of American children ages five to seventeen revealed that 64 percent of them fail to meet *minimum* fitness standards.

▶ Obesity among children six through eleven in this country is up by 54 percent since the 1960s, and super-obesity by as much as 98 percent, according to a 1987 study conducted by the Harvard School of Public Health.

▶ The average two- through five-year-old watches twenty-two hours of television per week.

▶ Fully 28 percent of our kids have high blood pressure, and nearly half have elevated levels of cholesterol; almost 70 percent eat too much salt; 75 percent have diets too rich in fats; and 67 percent show three or more risk factors for heart disease.

I could go on and on, but the bottom line is this: today's kids, our kids, are critically out of shape—even *dangerously* out of shape. As my friend Dr. Kenneth Cooper writes in his book *Kid Fitness:* "Millions of our children—the majority of them in middle- and upper-middle-class homes—face the prospect of serious diseases and shortened life spans because of sedentary living and poor nutrition. And the situation appears to be worsening."

Dr. Cooper and I both believe that this is a national crisis. And it is one that affects *you*, as the parent of a child in his early years, because this crisis is *progressive*. The millions of unfit high school students in this country, many of whom will become heart patients by the time they are fifty, are unfit as teenagers because nothing was done earlier in their lives to put them onto a lifetime fitness track. That track begins in the home, with parents who care about their children's future health and happiness; and *it can and should begin the moment your child is born.*

Many parents don't know that they can do a great deal in the child's first five years to give her a real head start toward lifelong fitness and to cut her chances of becoming yet another victim of America's youth fitness crisis. The purpose of this book is to make that knowledge public, and to provide you with everything you need to know to allow your infant, toddler, or preschooler to get a good start on his or her lifetime fitness track.

what is youth fitness, anyway, and why is it so important?

The American Alliance of Health, Physical Education, Recreation and Dance (AAHPERD) defines physical fitness as: "A physical state of well-being that allows people to perform daily activities with vigor, reduce their risk of health problems related to lack of exercise, and to establish a fitness base for participation in a variety of physical activities."

AAHPERD goes on to identify four basic, testable components of "health-related" physical fitness among children. They are: **body composition**, which is the measure of how fat or lean a person is; **cardiorespiratory endurance**, which is the capacity (known as *aerobic*) of the heart, lungs, and circulatory system to do moderate- to high-intensity exercise or work over an extended period of time; **flexibility**, which is the capacity to move joints and muscles freely through their full ranges of motion; and **muscular strength** and **endurance**, which is the capacity of the muscles both to do short-term forceful work and to work continuously and effectively over a period of time.

Put simply, a child who is physically fit for good health is not overly fat, has a strong, efficient cardiorespiratory system, and strong, flexible muscles that don't tire quickly. Elaborating on that definition, we could say that a child (or adult) fit for good health also practices smart nutrition, controls stress, and does not misuse drugs, tobacco, or alcohol.

This kind of health-related fitness produces so many benefits that it is almost like a magic potion. Fit kids are healthier and happier kids. They have better posture, sleep better, recover more quickly from illness and injury, are more resistant to sickness and injury, have more endurance, and can handle physical emergencies more easily than unfit kids. They *move* better and enjoy movement more—everything from sports to dance to going to and from class. They are mentally more alert, concentrate better, and, according to numerous studies, perform better at academics than unfit kids. And finally, fit kids are likely to become and remain fit adults, which means extended good health and longer life. (We know that physically inactive adults, for example, are almost *twice* as likely to develop coronary heart disease—the leading cause of death and disability in the United States—than adults who engage in regular physical activity.)

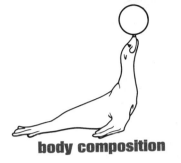

body composition

cardiorespiratory endurance

flexibility

muscular strength

muscular endurance

What parent would *not* want all this for his or her child? As I travel around the country in my position as chairman of the President's Council on Physical Fitness and Sports, I am often asked by parents *why* it is so important for kids to be fit, especially young kids. My answer is simple: because both the length and the quality of your child's life depend on it.

To answer that question in another way, let me ask *you* a question: if there was something you could go out and buy for your child that would make him or her far healthier, happier, and better prepared to deal with life than he or she would be without this thing, wouldn't you sell whatever you had to sell, do whatever you had to do, to get it? Well, there is such a thing—fitness. I believe it is the most valuable and important gift you can give your child.

okay, arnold, so what do we do?

Building a life of fitness and good health for and with your child is a little like building a house. The foundation should be started at birth and be in place by the time the child is six years old. The first floor is put in between ages six and ten, and the second floor is added between ages eleven and fourteen. You can't add the second floor until the first floor is in place. And if the house is going to be strong and lasting, you shouldn't start the first floor until you have a good foundation under it.

In my *Arnold's Fitness for Kids Ages 6–10* and *Ages 11–14,* I show you and your child how to build the first and second floors of lifetime fitness. In this book, we will concentrate on the foundation, which is made up of good nutrition and the development of basic physical skills, such as coordination, balance, agility, throwing, kicking, catching, etc. These skills not only are a prerequisite for perform-

ing well at sports later on in a child's life, but also provide kids with a good "movement base" from which they can effectively take up a wide range of fitness and recreational activities throughout their lives.

Youth fitness, from birth well into the teen years, *is* family fitness. *The best single thing you can do to cause your child to care about fitness, and to continue to care about it throughout his or her life, is to make exercise, physical activity, and good nutrition normal and indispensable parts of your family life from the time the child is born.* A child raised *into* these practices from birth is much more likely to internalize them and continue them into his or her adult life than one who is not.

A commitment to family fitness means a long-term commitment to involvement on your part. A 1988 study by the Melpomene Institute showed that one of the three most important influences on a child's involvement in exercise and physical activity is the time parents spend doing those things *with* the child. I know you're busy. So am I, but I find at least thirty minutes every day to play and exercise with my two daughters, and so can you. When you think about it, what could you possibly be doing for that half hour each day that is more important? Besides, family fitness is wonderful fun, and it provides unique opportunities from birth onward for developing closer relationships with your kids throughout their childhoods.

According to the Melpomene Institute, another critical influence on the types of exercise and physical activity habits your child develops (or doesn't develop) is your own exercise and physical activity habits.

As child psychiatrist Paul Gabriel has written: "The best and easiest way to motivate your child to stay fit is to stay fit yourself. The main reason children are out of shape is that they have poor role models. By making fitness a part of your life, you teach your child to value it."

What you do or don't do *counts* with your kids. It is almost impossible to convince children not to smoke and drink if you do those things yourself. Similarly, you'll be much more effective in getting your children to become conscious of what and how they eat if you're not always pigging out on doughnuts yourself, and more successful in getting them to exercise if they see you exercising regularly and enjoying it.

So my first three strong recommendations on how to begin laying the foundation for your child's future fitness and good health are:

▶ From the time your child is born, make your home and family ones in which exercise, shared physical activity, and smart eating are indispensable parts of everyday life.

▶ Do physical activities, exercises, and play *with* your kids, from birth right on through their childhoods.

▶ Practice what you preach: make yourself an example for your child of the life benefits of fitness.

My fourth recommendation is this:

make fitness fun.

The fact is that using and exercising our bodies and nourishing them well *are* fun—the greatest fun there is, I believe. But you have to find ways to demonstrate that fun to kids. Forget about getting them to exercise because it is "good for you." It won't work. What does work is to make your family play and exercise sessions imaginative and enjoyable from the very beginning. Do that, and your kids will run to them, rather than away from them.

how you should use this book

This book is about preparing your infants, toddlers, and preschoolers for a healthy, physically active life, *not* about putting them onto structured and systematic exercise regimens. This is not a fitness textbook, full of charts, tables, medical terms, and exercise routines—but a hands-on workbook that is meant to be used by you and your child together.

We have tried to make the book appealing-looking to young children, and I have included in it a series of children's stories about my early childhood in Austria, with my family and friends as other characters. These stories are interspersed between the book's chapters, and may be read to your child separately as individual stories relating to fitness and good health, or together as a small children's book. Either way, these stories will make a nice bedtime read to your children.

Preparation for youth fitness (or what Bob Glover and Jack Shepherd, authors of *The Family Fitness Handbook,* call "prefitness for preschoolers") starts for infants (from birth to age one) with good nutrition and parental encouragement of movement leading toward the development of basic physical, or "motor," skills. It continues for toddlers (ages one to three) and preschoolers (ages three through five) with physically active play and games and fun skill-development exercises and drills.

In Chapter 1, I explain what motor skills are and why developing a good base of these skills as early and thoroughly as possible is so important to fitness, sports participation, and lifetime physical aptitude. This chapter then describes the various stages of physical, skills, and learning development that a child goes through from infancy through five years old. It identifies the important basic motor skills and tells you at what ages your child is capable of acquiring them. And it tells you what you can do to assist your child (as an infant, a toddler, and a preschooler) with that acquisition by referring you to lists (one for each age group) of games, exercises, play activities, and skill drills (in the Appendix), all of them designed to be appealing to kids and fun for you and your child to do together.

Chapter 2 is a guide to good nutrition for infants, toddlers, and preschoolers. If the development of physical skills and a love of move-

ment is one half the foundation of your child's preparation for fitness and good health, smart and healthful eating is the other half. This chapter will tell you what you need to know to provide your child with the right diet for growth and good health and to make "eating smart" a permanent part of your family life.

Finally, Chapter 3 deals with the role preschool, kindergarten, and community programs can play in your child's "prefitness" life.

The first five years of human life are a precious and irrecoverable time—a time when children are most impressionable, a time when the basic patterns of motor skills that will serve a child for his or her entire life are either learned or not learned. If a child learns before age six to love movement, that love—translated into physical activity and exercise—can bring a lifetime of joy, vigor, and good health. As I said earlier, I believe the most valuable gift you can possibly give your child is a lifetime commitment to fitness and good health, and this book can help you build a strong foundation for that commitment.

when arnold was young

I grew up in Austria, in a very small village called Thal. Only eight hundred people lived in Thal, and most everyone lived on farms. All around the village were pastures and meadows and rolling hills where cows and horses grazed on sweet grass. There also were fields of wheat and hay and many orchards where cherries and apples and pears grew. Beyond the village and farmland were forests and mountains and streams. One stream ran all the way down a mountain, through the village and into a lake that was close to my home.

I lived in a very small house with my father and mother and brother. My father, whose name was Gustav, was a policeman, so we did not live on a farm. But our neighbors were farmers, and cows and chickens and horses, and many other kinds of farm animals, lived all around us, so that it was just like living on a farm.

We had electricity, but only for a few lights and a radio. The radio was very important to my family because we didn't own a television. In fact, there was only one television in the entire village. It was in a restaurant that only tourists went to. At night my father and mother and brother and I would sit around the radio and listen to the news and sporting events. My brother's name was Meinhard and he was a year older than me.

Our house was heated with wood- and coal-burning stoves. My mother, whose name is Aurelia, cooked our food in special tile ovens that were just like the ones used in castles. The stoves and ovens, which also burned coal, had to be cleaned of ash all the time, and I remember that it was a big job. My mother cleaned them by herself until Meinhard and I were old enough to help and eventually clean them without her. Meinhard and I also split and stacked the wood and carried the coal when we were older. It was hard work, but we didn't mind because we made a contest out of who could cut the most wood and carry the most coal.

But the hardest job of all was getting water. We didn't have indoor plumbing in our house, and we had to carry our water in pails from a well that was two hundred yards away. When we needed water for cooking or cleaning, we went to the well and pumped it up from deep in the ground. In winter we would trudge through the snow to the well, and the water in the pail would be turning to ice by the time we got it back to the house. In summer we used more water than in winter, because we had to water our vegetable garden every day. The most work of all was on wash day, when my mother washed our clothes. It took a full hour to bring in enough water to fill the washtub. My mother and brother and I would go back and forth between the well and the washroom with pails of water many times. Then, after a fire had been built under the tub and the clothes were "cooked" clean, they had to be rinsed with more water from the well. Even though carrying that much water was hard work, Meinhard and I had fun, because we made a contest of seeing who could carry the most pails. And no matter how tired I was, I always made sure I carried more than my brother.

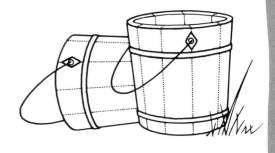

FiTNeSS

1 what you can do to prepare your infant, toddler, and preschooler for lifetime fitness

building the skills base

Physical, or "motor," skills are the building blocks of all bodily movement. Every coordinated movement that we make with our bodies is based on a motor skill, or a number of motor skills put together. We begin acquiring motor skills from the moment we are born, and those earliest skills—such as

grasping, reaching, sucking—become the first building blocks for all our future movements. As he or she grows, an infant acquires more and more of these skills and begins to put them together in different combinations, and to substitute one for another, in order to create new patterns of movement that can be used in response to different stimuli.

The motivation for an infant to acquire many skills, and to experiment with them in various increasingly complex combinations, is a direct result of the amount, kind, and quality of stimulation the infant receives. That is a very important sentence for parents! More primary motor skills are acquired during the first two years of life than at any other time, and many experts believe that *all* the primary motor skills a person will ever have are acquired by age ten. (According to these experts, skills acquired after age ten are modifications and new combinations of the primary skills an individual already has.) What this means is—and this is another very important sentence for parents—*the more comprehensively and effectively a child is stimulated during the first five years of life, the greater the number and sophistication of motor skills that child will develop (within the limitations of his or her genetic endowment).*

Why is the development of motor skills so important? Because they form the foundation of all of a person's physical activity for the rest of that person's life. There are many adult Americans who are physically inactive because as children they never acquired the skills that would have allowed them to do and enjoy sports and other physical activities. In other words, motor skills have quite a lot to do with health-related fitness—you have to have a good skills base in order to perform many health-related fitness activities and exercises.

Dr. Bob Arnot, founder of the Lake Placid Winter Olympic Training Lab, and coauthor of the book *SportsTalent,* has said:
"Building a good skills base for a child as early as possible is the most important single step a parent can take to insure that child's long-term health and fitness."

And Professor Vern Seefeldt, director of the Youth Sports Institute at Michigan State University, writes: "The focus of children's fitness should be on developing motor skills. Running, hopping, jumping, skipping, throwing, catching, and kick-

ing are the ABCs of movement. We found that when children have these skills, fitness and sports are second nature. Most children just haven't mastered movement, and so they are reluctant to move."

If a good skills foundation is important to the performance of health-related fitness activities and exercise, it is absolutely *crucial* to the performance and enjoyment of sports. No one enjoys doing things they cannot do well, and that is particularly true of sports. If you start playing baseball with some of your friends and find out you can't bat or catch or throw well, the chances are good you won't play baseball for very long, and you will probably never come back to it later on in life. If you begin playing baseball with good throwing, catching, and batting skills, however, you will perform better at the sport, enjoy it more, and very likely stay with it.

The development of physical skills has considerable importance in areas other than sports and fitness. Variety and sophistication of motor skills are acquired in activities as disparate as flying an airplane, ballet dancing, sculpting, driving a race car, and performing surgery; and a person without motor skills variety and sophistication will most likely be unable to utilize his or her abilities in a broad spectrum of human activities.

No parent wants a child to grow up clumsy, or to suffer from low self-esteem because of klutziness, or to be unable to do the thousands of enjoyable things in life that require coordination, deftness, and physical grace. Yet very few American parents make any real effort to encourage motor skills development in their kids, particularly at the time in their kids' lives when that development is most important. Between birth and age six is *the* time in the child's life when parents should do everything they can to encourage and stimulate the building of a good, broad base of fundamental physical skills, ones that will give their kids access for the rest of their lives to sports, fitness activities, and the pleasures of efficient physical movement.

So how do you help your child develop a broad base of sophisticated motor skills? First, by understanding that *readiness* is the key to skills attainment.

Every child goes through a normal developmental sequence in the acquisition of basic skills. For example, a child has to master sitting up before he can pivot without falling, before he can stand while holding on to something, before he can walk with assistance. And he must do *all* these things, in sequence, before he can finally walk by himself. Kids will progress through motor skills sequences at various learning speeds, and chronological age has very little to do with exactly when a skill can be acquired.

But readiness has everything to do with it. Remember this: *you cannot teach your child a new skill until he or she is ready to learn it.* Being ready means that the child (1) has mastered the skills that must be learned before learning the new one; (2) has a mature enough motor and sensory system to be able to perform the new skill; and (3) *wants* to learn the new skill. A child simply cannot walk, no matter how much you encourage her to, if she has not yet learned the skills subordinate to walking, if her spinal cord is not yet developed enough to allow her to walk, and/or if she doesn't yet want to walk.

What this means is that you the parent should take advantage of each stage of skills development in your child's life as it comes, making sure the child masters as wide a variety of skills at that stage as possible, instead of trying to rush the child through a sequence of skills toward a particular goal, such as walking or riding a bicycle.

Here's an example of what I'm talking about. Let's say you'd like for your child eventually to play and enjoy baseball. The best way to encourage and stimulate the skills he'll need to do that is not to suddenly start playing baseball with him when he is five years old, but to begin much earlier to develop the individual skills that underline and precede baseball skills. You should practice them one at a time, within your child's attention span and abilities, and loudly approve the acquisition of each new skill. Some of the sequential building-block skills for batting, for example, would be hitting a large stationary ball on the ground, then hitting a large ball rolled on the ground, then a large ball in the air, then a soft-pitched large ball, a soft-pitched smaller ball, etc. The visual tracking skills that allow an older child to hit a baseball can go back to their development at the infancy stage, with a parent moving a ball slowly backward and forward and from side to side in front of a baby's face.

Here are a few other general but important things you can do to help your child begin building a solid skills base:

► Create an overall environment in your home that will interest your child from birth onward in physical movement and movement awareness. Make the joy of graceful, efficient movement an intrinsic part of your family life and engage your child in that joy —with movement, crib toys and games, play, and by dancing and roughhousing with her. There are no rules for how to do this— it is up to your intuition and imagination as a parent.

▶ Make skills development fun at all times; never let it seem like work to your child. Keep your skill-building sessions short and enjoyable.

▶ Spend creative time with your child breaking down various skills into individual units of movement that will interest the child and hold his or her attention.

▶ The more you know about the physiological and mental development of your infant, toddler, or preschooler, the better. Read the information on development in this chapter carefully and keep it in mind as you work with your child.

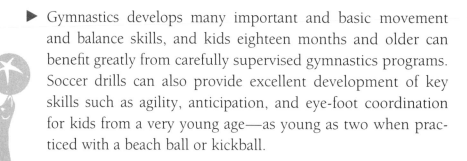

▶ Gymnastics develops many important and basic movement and balance skills, and kids eighteen months and older can benefit greatly from carefully supervised gymnastics programs. Soccer drills can also provide excellent development of key skills such as agility, anticipation, and eye-foot coordination for kids from a very young age—as young as two when practiced with a beach ball or kickball.

a note about development

As I have said, a child has to be ready to acquire any new skill. In the following section on skill acquisition for infants, toddlers, and preschoolers, I provide you with lists of basic motor skills, along with the ages at which those skills are normally acquired by children. You should remember that no two children develop, or acquire skills, at exactly the same rate, and these skill-acquisition milestones should be viewed by parents as rough guidelines, not precise indicators, as to where your child should be at a particular point in his or her life. If your child is a little fast or slow in reaching these milestones, you needn't worry, but if your child is consistently behind in these acquisition schedules, and/or cannot perform many of the skills appropriate for his or her age, you should consult with your pediatrician.

For parents who might want in-depth information about the physical, cognitive, and emotional development of infants, toddlers, and preschoolers, I recommend the authoritative and comprehensive volume put out by the American Academy of Pediatrics called *Caring for Your Baby and Young Child: Birth to Age 5,* edited by Steven Shelov, M.D. It can be ordered from the Academy, P.O. Box 927, Elk Grove Village, IL 60007, telephone (800) 433-9016.

I. infant development and skill acquisition

The first year of your child's life is one of explosive growth and change. Within that year a child's brain and stomach nearly triple in size, the heart nearly doubles, the lungs more than double, and the child triples his or her birthweight. By the end of the first year, your baby will be crawling, sitting without assistance, standing without support, and possibly walking. He or she will be able to pick things up with the thumb and forefinger, put objects into a container and take them out again, imitate words, say "Mama" and "Dada," and use simple gestures to communicate. During the course of all this growth and learning, there is much that

you can do to stimulate your baby to love movement and to encourage the acquisition of skills and body awareness through directed play.

Play is the key word here. I don't recommend exercise regimens for infants, or even a systematic skills development program, but rather, regular and frequent physical contact with your baby, and lots of movement-oriented play that allows the infant as many and varied opportunities as possible to master new physical skills. As Dr. Kenneth Cooper has written: "The more you encourage your child to be physically active during this period, the stronger and more energetic you can expect him to become, and the more quickly he'll develop skills in using his muscles."

In the Appendix to this book, you will find a list of "play exercises" and games for infants that are especially designed to encourage the development of various basic skills. I strongly recommend that you use these activities, but be sure to make them fun and never overtax your baby with them. Each child has his or her own rhythm of growth and development and changes in mood, and his or her readiness to try new things will be apparent to you. Whenever doing one of these activities with your baby seems to have lost its appeal, or if the baby becomes fussy, it's time to stop for that day. There will be plenty of other days when the activity will regain its appeal. The main thing to remember is never to make these activities into scheduled "work" for your baby; keep your sessions brief, spontaneous, and well within the context of play.

The list of motor skills "milestones" at the end of this section will give you an idea of which skills are best encouraged during each quarter of your baby's first year; I have also added a list

of toys that can help with that encouragement. But first, here are some general guidelines on how to effectively introduce skill-developing, movement-encouraging play into your infant's life:

▶ Do physical activity with your baby when she is happy and either quietly or actively alert, not when she is drowsy or crying. Try shaking a rattle near your baby's ear to get her attentive and ready for play.

▶ Don't coop up your baby. Right from birth give your infant plenty of freedom to move around. Loose clothing, a big playpen, a "babyproofed" room (as soon as the child can crawl), all encourage movement rather than stifle it.

▶ The more your baby moves, the better. Gently move her arms and legs around; help her to roll over; as of about four to six months, allow her to push with her legs against the floor or against you; encourage her to hold on to your fingers and pull herself up toward you; after about six months, start holding her in a standing position and walking her around; hold toys just out of reach and make the baby reach, stretch, and then grasp. The more movement and the more varied the movement at this age, the more your baby will come to love it.

▶ As of about two months, give your baby various manageable soft toys to handle—to practice grasping, picking up, and banging together. Toys hung overhead in the crib will stimulate batting and grabbing.

▶ Babies as young as one month can focus briefly on objects as far away as three feet, but prefer to focus on objects between eight and fifteen inches in front of them. To help a baby develop visual tracking skills, move your head slowly from side to side as you hold him, and move bright objects (babies love red) up and down and from side to side at various distances from his face and at different speeds. A mobile hung over his crib is a good way to stimulate a young infant's vision, but mobiles should be removed by the time your baby is able to pull himself upright. You can also stretch a bar across the baby's playpen or crib and hang various bright objects from it for the baby to focus on. Blow bubbles for your baby to track and reach for, and shine a flashlight beam on a wall, moving it back and forth and around in circles for the baby to watch.

► You can start rolling balls to your baby early on—it helps her develop visual tracking and convergence skills. At around four to six months, she should start batting at the balls, and by the end of her first year, she should be rolling them back. Balls of various sizes (none small enough to swallow) are great toys for babies and can be used to encourage lots of different skills.

► Once your baby is strong enough to raise his chest off the floor, start helping him to practice sitting up. Hold him in a sitting position or prop him up in a corner of the couch while he learns to balance himself. Bright objects or toys put in front of him will give him something to focus on while he works on his balance.

► After about six months, the development of fine-muscle movement skills becomes important. You should encourage your baby to use her hands as much as possible—by letting her feed herself (even though it's messy), draw with crayons, play with multipart and moving-part toys, and similar activities. Before six months, encourage your baby to handle stuffed animals or soft dolls, cloth, plastic, or wooden blocks (from about four months on), and household objects such as wooden spoons and blunt spatulas, plastic cups and dishes, pots, pans, and empty boxes.

► To encourage your child to crawl (usually between seven and ten months), try putting interesting objects on the floor just out of his reach. Once he has started crawling, set up obstacle courses of pillows and cushions for him to crawl over and around.

► Baby walkers actually slow the process of learning to walk, and can be dangerous for infants and toddlers as well. For these reasons, I urge you not to use them. When helping your child to learn to walk, support her around the trunk or hold the back of her clothing, to allow her to have her arms free for balancing.

► Don't ever use the television as a pacifier for your child.

motor skills milestones in your child's first year

NOTE: Remember, these are *general* guidelines, meant to give you an idea of when you can most effectively encourage specific skills. Don't worry if your baby is a little ahead of or behind these schedules. Check them off as your child reaches each of these milestones.

by three months old, your baby

- ☐ moves each arm and each leg equally well.

- ☐ follows slowly moving objects with eyes.

- ☐ starts using hands and eyes in coordination.

- ☐ stretches legs out and kicks while lying down.

- ☐ swipes with hands at objects dangling above or in front of him.

- ☐ shakes and grasps hand toys.

by six months old, your baby

- ☐ can roll over from stomach to back or vice versa.

- ☐ can sit with support of hands and then without hand support.

- ☐ can reach with one hand.

- ☐ can play with hands by touching them together.

- ☐ can see and pick up small objects like crumbs.

- ☐ can bring objects to mouth.

- ☐ can try to get out-of-reach objects.

- ☐ can track faster-moving objects with his eyes, like a ball rolled across the floor.

by nine months old, your baby

- ☐ can support weight on outstretched hands while on stomach.

- ☐ can sit without support.

- ☐ can creep (dragging body along floor).

- ☐ can hold bottle unassisted.

- ☐ can transfer objects from hand to hand.

- ☐ can get from crawling to sitting position.

- ☐ can stand by pushing self up.

- ☐ can rake objects to himself with hand.

- ☐ can grab a moving object, like a ball rolled in front of him.

by twelve months old, your baby

- ☐ can crawl well on hands and knees with stomach clear of floor.

- ☐ can climb stairs on hands, knees, and feet.

- ☐ can stand briefly without support.

- ☐ can walk while holding on to furniture, and maybe entirely without support.

- ☐ can bang two objects together.

- ☐ can grasp objects accurately with the thumb and forefinger or second finger.

- ☐ can put objects into a container and take them out.

toys for infants that help develop skills and encourage movement

up to eight months

☐ Mobiles in bright colors and contrasting patterns

☐ Unbreakable mirrors attached to inside of crib and/or playpen

☐ Activity quilts

☐ Music boxes and musical toys, such as bells, drums, or tambourines

☐ Rattles and other hand toys (none so small it can be swallowed)

☐ "Busy" boxes

☐ Soft balls of different sizes (none small enough to fit in mouth)

☐ Jumper seat for hanging and bouncing in doorways

☐ Baby books, crayons, drawing paper

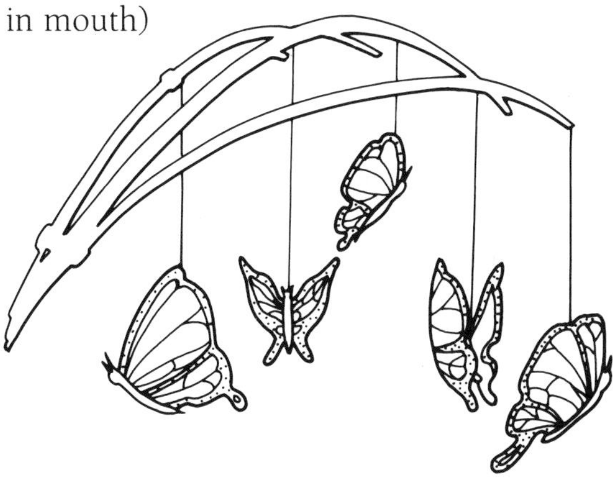

eight to twelve months

☐ Stacking toys in different colors, sizes, and shapes

☐ Building blocks

☐ Bath toys

☐ Push-pull toys

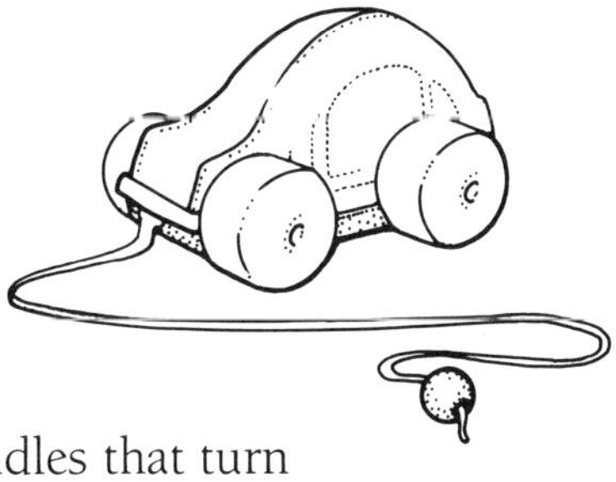

☐ Toys with moving parts, handles that turn

☐ Pails, cups, and other containers and things to put into them and take out of them

☐ Picture and drawing books, crayons, musical toys, and musical boxes

II. toddler development and skill acquisition

The second and third years of your child's life—the toddler years—are years of growing independence and of tremendous physical, emotional, intellectual, and social changes. In this period, your child will go from a completely dependent infant, unable to talk and barely able to walk, to an irrepressible little perpetual-motion machine. At this age, he can speak in four- to five-word sentences, understand most of what is said to him, and is perfectly capable of thinking and acting for himself and of totally ignoring you. (During the "terrible twos," many children seem to enjoy testing their new independence by trying to pretend their parents don't exist!)

By his third birthday, your child will likely have grown to half his adult height. His baby fat will be disappearing and he will look stronger and leaner than he did even six months ago.

Ideally, during the past two years (his second and third), he has come to love movement and physical activity; his nutrition has been good; his muscles have gotten strong from exercise; and he has developed a solid base of fundamental motor skills that allow him to learn new physical activities quickly and easily, and to perform a wide variety of sophisticated movements. This is where you want your child to be on his third birthday. Now let's look at how you will help get him there.

The major physical accomplishment of your child's second year will be learning to walk and perfecting that skill—and while you shouldn't try to rush your child into walking before she is ready, there is much you can do to help her perfect this crucial new skill once she has acquired it. Walking around objects, up and down stairs, backward, up and down "mountains" of sofa cushions, and so forth, can all be fun—interactive games between you and your toddler that will quickly improve her walking skills and prepare her for the burst of physical activity that happens in the third year.

Between two and three, your child may seem to be continually climbing, jumping, running, kicking; and all this activity—particularly if it is partially directed by you—is wonderful for strengthening her body and developing basic movement skills.

As with infants, any movement encouragement and skills development done with kids ages one and two should be kept strictly within the context of play. Also remember that the attention span of one- and two-year-olds is very short; any directed "play exercises" and games such as the ones given for toddlers in the Appendix should be done with a child only in brief sessions and only so long as the child *enjoys* them. Don't forget that your goal is to nurture in your child a *love* of movement and physical activity that will lead to a lifetime of fitness. The surest way to have the *opposite* effect is to force exercise onto very young children, or to turn movement into work.

It should also be said that kids in this age range (particularly the two-year-olds) are learning and beginning to learn skills that "provide the groundwork for later, more complex abilities that are essential to the enjoyment and the efficient performance of exercise," as Dr. Ken Cooper has put it. Cooper adds: "If your child can learn [these skills] at an early age, he'll also be more likely to build on them at an early age. This means that he'll become more adept at playground activities, at pick-up games during recess and physical education class, and later, at team sports." You can do a lot to help your child get off to a good skills start during these years by turning skill-development activities into play and by participating in that play with your child on a regular basis. The games and "play exercises" in the back of this book are designed to help you do that.

Once again, I have included at the end of this section a list of motor skills "milestones" to give you an idea of which skills are best encouraged at ages one and two. But first, here are some general recommendations for how to get your toddler enthusiastically involved in skill-developing physical activity:

► Between ages one and two is a crucial time for developing hand-eye coordination. Make sure your one-year-old has plenty of toys—like easy jigsaw puzzles, blocks, connecting toys such as peg-boards and shape sorters, and moving-part toys—that aid that development. (Other good skill-development toys for one-year-olds are balls of various sizes, pushing and pulling toys, a beginner's tricycle, and a plastic bat to practice hitting big balls.) Some games that help develop hand-eye coordination and hand and finger skills are picking up or batting rolled balls, turning knobs and pages, scribbling and drawing, putting pegs into holes, folding paper, building with blocks, and putting objects into and taking them out of containers.

► Make up fun and safe obstacle walks for your toddler and let him follow you around chairs, tables, over cushions; outside, you can use trees, curbs, bushes, and mailboxes to make your walks into "follow me" adventures.

► Kids of this age love roughhousing. Wrestling on the bed or in a pile of leaves, "flying" the child overhead, piggyback rides—all these things cause kids to love movement and to be adventurous about trying new movements. The more running, climbing, sliding, hopping, skipping, somersaulting, and rolling your games with your toddler include, the better.

► Once your child has started walking, it is a good idea to have a given room, or part of a room, in your house "childproofed" and turned into a play area. If you have the space outside, it is also a good idea to have an outdoor play area. At the end of this chapter, I will give you some suggestions on how to set up great, safe indoor and outdoor play areas cheaply and simply.

► It is usually in these years that Fitness Enemy Number One, The TV, first rears its ugly head. I suggest you come up now with a television watching schedule for your child (in my house it is five hours a week) that you can stick with through elementary school. If a child becomes accustomed early on to the fact that other activities in your household, including physical activity, have a higher priority than TV, it will be much easier later to control his or her TV watching. Remember, the average two- to five-year-old in America watches *twenty-two hours of TV a week*. Just think how much healthier our kids would be if all that time were given over to exercise and play!

► The primary sports-related skills are catching, throwing, striking (as with a bat or a racquet), and kicking. Start practicing these skills with your child as soon as he or she is ready to try them, and find as many fun ways to practice them as possible. (Lots of games that enlist these skills are given in the Appendix, but use your imagination to come up with others.)

motor skills milestones in your child's second and third years

NOTE: Remember, these are *general* guidelines, meant to give you an idea of when to encourage specific skills. Don't worry if your child is a little ahead of or behind these schedules. Check them off as your child reaches each of these milestones.

by two years old, your child

☐ walks forward and backward unassisted.

☐ walks up and down stairs holding on to support.

☐ can carry several small objects or one large object while walking.

☐ can stand on tiptoes.

☐ has begun to run.

☐ can jump with a one-foot takeoff.

☐ can kick a ball.

☐ can build towers of four or more blocks.

☐ can scribble.

☐ can put round pegs into holes.

by three years old, your child

☐ can climb well.

☐ can walk up and down stairs alternating feet.

☐ can jump with a two-foot takeoff.

☐ runs easily.

- ☐ can hop on one foot.

- ☐ can roll a ball.

- ☐ can throw a ball underhand with one or two hands.

- ☐ can kick a ball well.

- ☐ can strike an object with hand, overarm, or sidearm.

- ☐ pedals a tricycle.

- ☐ can push and pull a person or object.

- ☐ can balance on one foot for three to five seconds.

- ☐ can walk several steps on a one-inch-wide straight line.

- ☐ can walk a four-inch-wide beam alternating feet.

- ☐ can screw and unscrew jar lids, or similar objects, and turn rotating handles.

- ☐ can make vertical, circular, and horizontal strokes with a crayon.

- ☐ can build towers of more than six blocks.

III. preschooler development and skill acquisition

During the fourth, fifth, and sixth years of your child's life, his or her nervous system develops enough to provide the cognitive foundation necessary to begin making effective use of the physical skills the child has already developed and is still developing. You will see budding interest in trying new activities, learning new skills, participating in games, and even following rules. During this time, your child will learn sophisticated balancing skills; how to catch, bat, and throw a ball overhand; how to slide and gallop and skip. He or she will also learn how to consciously put skills together to create new skills; how to employ those skills in games; and how to understand and follow the rules of those games. Moreover, children in this age range can and

should start drawing on the skills base they already have to begin learning lifetime fitness activities such as riding a bike, swimming, cross-country and downhill skiing, roller and/or ice skating, and tennis.

As with infants and toddlers, it is crucially important for parents not to overtax or bore their preschoolers with systematic exercise programs or skills development regimens. It is equally important, however, for parents to make sure that skills development and exercise continue to be offered to a child as *play*— offered in brief, fun sessions, with the parents always participating as playmates, cheerleaders, and trainers.

Many children in this age range enjoy group games and play with other kids, and you might find that your child is more enthusiastic about your "exercise sessions" if you bring other kids into them from time to time.

In any case, I recommend that from your child's third birthday onward, you institute a regular family "play period" of ten to twenty minutes a day, at least five days a week. (I know you're busy, but you can make the time.)

Set up a "play room," or play area, in your house or apartment, and/or a play area outside (I tell you how to do that at the end of this chapter), and let those places be your "gym." Try to go there at a regular time each day (pick a time when your child is not tired or hungry or cranky) and "play," using the "play exercises" and games for preschoolers given in the Appendix of this book, and/or games and exercises that you and your child invent. The point is to spend time doing physical activities with your child that build muscles, flexibility, and stamina; that develop and improve physical skills; and that foster—because they are *fun*

and done with *you*—your child's enjoyment of movement and exercise. Mix up the games and exercises to keep the sessions from getting stale and predictable, and every two weeks or so, go out to a park or playground, a beach or a lake, for your play period.

Helping your child to put her developing skills together into various effective "motor programs," so that she feels physically capable and confident, is a job best done in the home. But once your three- or four-year-old has gained some physical confidence, you may want to introduce her to an organized play group or a preschool exercise program. In Chapter 3, I will offer some guidelines to help you make that decision, and describe a few such programs.

Your three-year-old may be just as active as he was at two, but his attention span should be longer and his ability to concentrate, better. This means that he can play at individual games longer without getting bored, and can sustain interest in interactive games such as tag and catch, either with you or with other kids.

Many kids go through a difficult period between ages four and five, characterized by dramatic mood swings, bossiness, belligerence, and general orneriness. Your child may decide during this time that he's not interested in your family play periods anymore. Fine—just wait him out and use your imagination to come up with ways to keep him active. Remember, you are cutting off your nose to spite your face if you try to force a child, *particularly* a four-year-old, to exercise or practice skills.

Normal four- and five-year-olds have almost all the coordination, balance, agility, and manual dexterity of an adult. While skill-development and skill-refinement activities are still very important, it is also important to begin introducing kids at this age to health-related fitness activities, such as vigorous aerobic play, stretching, and games and "play exercises" that strengthen muscles and build stamina. If you have helped your child build a good skills base, this introduction to health-related activities (for now, the kinds of games and play listed in the Appendix, and soon, more systematic exercise and organized sports) should be a smooth and pleasurable one.

Your child will probably enter kindergarten when he or she is five. That kindergarten may or may not offer a physical education program, and if it does, the program may or may not be a good one. To be a good one, the program should be taught by a physical education specialist. In any case, don't rely on it to substitute for your family play periods with your child. Similarly, if your five-year-old joins a T-ball or soccer league, or other preschool sports program, that program may be very good for his or her physical development, but it can't and shouldn't take the place of your family play sessions. The average five-year-old is still very much focused and dependent on his relationship with his parents. *You* are still the ones whose lead he follows, and it is crucially important that the family fitness you'll want to start practicing when your child turns six (see *Arnold's Fitness for Kids Ages 6–10*) be already well rooted in the enjoyment and security of directed family play. As I have said before, youth fitness *is* family fitness, and it begins right in your home with the activities you and your child do together. No program outside of the home can possibly substitute for that.

I have included at the end of this section a list of motor skills "milestones" that are normally reached by children of three, four, and five years of age. Some of the "play exercises" and games for preschoolers described in the Appendix are designed to develop and improve those skills; others are designed to strengthen muscles, build cardiovascular stamina, and keep your child's joints and muscles flexible. All are designed to be fun for you and your preschooler to do together, combining them however you like into ten- to twenty-minute play periods.

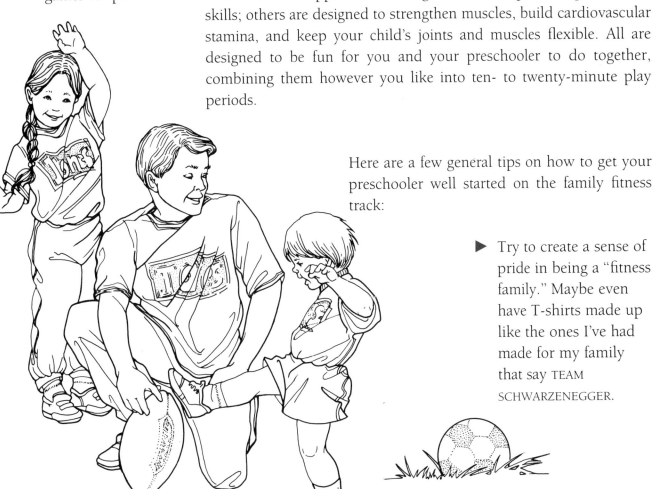

Here are a few general tips on how to get your preschooler well started on the family fitness track:

▶ Try to create a sense of pride in being a "fitness family." Maybe even have T-shirts made up like the ones I've had made for my family that say TEAM SCHWARZENEGGER.

► Limit TV watching. It robs the whole family of time you could be spending together playing and exercising. In my family we limit TV time to five hours a week, and we all choose together what those five hours will be.

► Set fun competitions and goals in your family play periods, and give out "awards" for realizing those goals or even for trying. Use your imagination to find ways to keep your play sessions fun, challenging, stress-free, and spontaneous.

► Teach your preschooler to *enjoy*, not avoid, physical work by including her in activities like raking leaves and shoveling snow. Encourage her to walk up stairs instead of using the escalator or elevator. Teach her early to enjoy *using* her body.

► Make your family vacations active ones. Activities like hiking, biking, canoeing, skating, cross-country skiing, swimming, and running, when begun before six years old in the fun context of a family vacation, often become lifetime fitness pursuits.

► Invent your own home "Bowl Games" and "Olympics" for your child and some of his friends—one in which everyone wins and has a good time.

► Three-year-olds still need plenty of hand and hand-eye skills development and refinement. Some quiet-time activities that will help with that are: pegboard and simple puzzles; building with blocks; coloring and scribbling; stringing beads together; taking apart and putting together multipart toys.

► As your preschooler is learning to count, reinforce this learning and let the child exercise at the same time. For example, take her outside or to the park and ask her to run and get you two blades of grass, then three leaves, four rocks, etc. To help learn colors at home on a rainy day, ask her to run and go get something red from the kitchen, hop and go get something blue from the living room, and so on.

motor skills milestones in your child's fourth, fifth, and sixth years

NOTE: Remember, these are *general* guidelines, meant to give you an idea of when specific skills are appropriately encouraged. Don't worry if your child is a little ahead of or behind these schedules. Check them off as your child reaches each of these milestones.

by four years old, your child

- ☐ can move backward and forward with agility.

- ☐ can somersault.

- ☐ can gallop.

- ☐ can slide sideways on both feet, as on ice.

- ☐ can throw a ball overhand.

- ☐ can catch by trapping a ball to chest.

- ☐ can catch a bounced ball most of the time.

- ☐ can throw a ball with elementary overarm methods.

- ☐ can bounce or dribble a ball with two hands.

- ☐ can strike an object sidearm with a bat or racquet.

- ☐ can balance on one foot for ten seconds.

- ☐ can walk a one-inch-wide circular line.

- ☐ can walk a two- to three-inch beam using alternating foot-over-foot steps.

- ☐ can use scissors.

- ☐ can draw circles and squares and can copy some letters.

by five years old, your child

☐ can swing, climb, skip, and jump skillfully.

☐ can do a backward somersault.

☐ can catch a ball using hands to grasp it.

☐ can kick a rolled ball, as in kickball or soccer.

☐ can probably dribble a ball with one hand.

☐ can strike an object with a bat or racquet with two-arm batting motion.

☐ can walk backward on a four-inch-wide board.

☐ may be riding a bicycle.

☐ can use table implements.

☐ can copy triangles and other geometric patterns.

by six years old, your child

☐ can hop on one foot skillfully.

☐ may be throwing, using mature overarm pattern.

☐ can catch a ball by letting it settle into the hands.

☐ can dribble a ball with feet, as in soccer.

☐ can punt (drop a ball and kick it in the air).

☐ can dribble a ball with one hand and walk at the same time.

☐ can support the body in the basic inverted position, as in a rudimentary headstand, with feet off the floor and knees on elbows.

☐ can hop on one foot proficiently.

☐ can stand on one foot with eyes closed for at least three seconds.

☐ can jump rope swung by two holders.

creating your own "home-dome" play area for toddlers and preschoolers

indoors

If you have a finished basement or a family room, you can create an indoor play area with a few simple pieces of equipment that are inexpensively bought and/or homemade. First of all, make sure there are no throw rugs kids can slip on if they are running. Put down good indoor/outdoor carpeting with a light padding underneath. Remove all unsafe breakables and put safety covers on all electrical outlets. Remove any standing lamps that could be toppled.

What you will need for starters is a large exercise mat for tumbling, exercising, etc. You can also get a cloth tube from a department store for crawling and tunneling through. Then you can make a slide out of an old couch and a leaf from an old dining room table (pad the edges that may scratch tender skin!). Tiny tots will love your help sliding down, and you can spot them while they climb back up (it could be slippery, so beware). Older sliders will know just what to do, but will still need supervision.

Here are some other suggestions:

cardboard boxes: the ones that appliances come in make great tunnels to crawl through, and also make good sections of obstacle courses.

rug samples (remnants): make excellent exercise mats.

beach balls: blow up two or three of them and have the kids chase them around and roll on them (always supervised!); then have the kids sit on the floor in a circle (or face to face, if there are just two of you), with legs spread so everyone's toes touch, and roll the ball back and forth to one another. There are many other games you can play with beach balls.

bubbles: blow bubbles for toddlers and walkers to chase around the room.

beanbag chairs or cushions: pile or strew these around the room and let the kids crawl up and down and over and around the soft mountains and valleys. Make them into obstacle courses to be crawled or run around.

balloons: turn loose a bunch of balloons and get the child or children to try to keep them all up in the air. Run after any balloon that's on the floor (before a snake gets it!) and throw it back up in the air. (Balloons can present choking and other hazards to small children when burst, so be sure that any play with balloons is well supervised.)

nerf or other foam toys: like the bat and ball and the basketball and goal—these are also great skill builders that can be used indoors or out.

If you want to get into more sophisticated play and fitness equipment for young kids, there are a number of catalogs that carry such things. Two (both free) are the Back to Basics Toys catalog, 8802 Monard Drive, Silver Spring, MD 20910, telephone (800) 356-5360; and for fine wooden outdoor play equipment, the catalog from Cedar Works, Route 1, Box 640, Rockport, ME 04856, telephone (800) 462-3327.

outdoors

You can set up a good outside play area in your yard without taking up much space or spending much money. Having the area fenced in is nice for unsupervised play, but not necessary for your family play periods.

A **jungle gym** is wonderful for outside play. Some lumberyards sell unfinished ones and/or kits that are reasonably priced, or you can build your own. The good ones are terrific multistation exercisers—with bars to hang and do pull-ups from, swings to swing on, rungs to climb on, slides to slide down, rings to swing upside down and flip over on, platforms to crawl under or climb over, a firemen's pole to slide down, and a horse swing to ride on with a friend. Every major muscle group can be exercised on a jungle gym.

An extra thick **rope** with knots tied in it about every twelve inches and hung from a tree can be a great climbing tool. Also, try tying a rope to the top of a slide, and let kids pull/walk themselves up the slide. Parental supervision is advised.

A **sandbox** is easy to build and wonderful fun for kids to push trucks and bulldozers around and build castles in.

You can make a **balance beam** by sanding down a weather-treated eight-foot length of two-by-four-inch board.

Old **bike tires** (and auto tires for older kids) laid together in different patterns make excellent "agility courses" for kids to walk, run, or hop through.

The classic **rope/tire swing** is great for swinging on and—when set to move slowly —as a target for throwing balls through.

You can buy a **tether ball** set at any major department store. A tall pole is placed in the ground and a ball is attached to it from a long cord. This game allows kids to get used to hitting a ball with their hands and also get used to it coming back to them to be hit again. They learn cause and effect (the harder the ball is hit, the faster it will whip around to them again), and their depth perception and dexterity can be enhanced. More than one child can use a tether ball game at a time.

Get your child started **juggling.** It is a great skills builder.

Frisbees, foam footballs, foam soft-balls and bats, mini-basketball goals, kickballs, beach balls, volleyballs, street-hockey sticks, jump ropes, Wiffle balls, Hula Hoops, a child-size badminton set, scarves or beanbags for juggling —these are all good, inexpensive toys for your outdoor play area.

when
arnold
was young

My mother was a very good cook who always prepared wholesome meals for our family. We ate potatoes and carrots and peas, and many other kinds of vegetables, from our garden, and picked lots of fruit from our neighbors' orchards. We stored our vegetables and fruits in a special room beneath our house. It had a dirt floor and was called a root cellar, and it was always dark and cool, like a refrigerator.

When I was four, I was allowed to help pick fruit in the orchards. My mother would take Meinhard and me to a neighbor's orchard in the fall and show us the correct way to pick apples and pears and cherries. She always insisted we first pick only the fruit that had no marks or bruises. This was because damaged fruit does not keep very long, and we tried to

pick enough fruit, especially apples, to last all winter. After the best time for picking had passed, we gathered fruit that had fallen to the ground. Even though it was bruised and would not last, my mother wanted it for preserving. She would cook the fruit and make delicious compotes, pies, and fillings.

Gathering fruit was always fun, because in the fall the air is cool and crisp and Meinhard and I could run through the orchards without getting tired. Sometimes we would play tag, sometimes we would play soldiers and throw rotten apples at each other from make-believe forts. And sometimes we ate so many apples that our stomachs ached and we couldn't eat our lunch.

NUTRiTiON

2 smart nutrition for your infant, toddler, and preschooler

As I said in the Introduction to this book, the development of physical skills and a love of movement is one half the foundation of your child's lifetime preparation for fitness and good health. The other half is good family nutrition— or what I call "eating smart."

Of the ten leading causes of death in America, five—athero- sclerosis, stroke, heart disease, diabetes, and cancer—can be

caused by bad diet. High blood pressure, obesity, and osteoporosis can also be caused by what and how much you eat. Eating dumb, in short, can make us sick, and even kill us. It also robs us of energy, makes our bodies soft and fat, and keeps us from performing well at sports, at school, and on the job. And this is every bit as true for kids as it is for adults. Like exercise, good nutrition is a habit, and the earlier it is begun in a child's life, the better.

In this chapter, I will give you some general guidelines for infant, toddler, and preschooler nutrition, and then some tips on how you can incorporate smart eating into your family life. Just as parent participation is crucial to getting kids to exercise, parents *have* to eat smart themselves if they want their kids to do so. It just won't work to tell little Tommy to lay off the jelly doughnuts if he sees you sneaking them every time you get a chance.

Eating smart is first of all knowing what is good for you and what is not. Then it is the simple discipline of practicing that knowledge in the form of good eating habits until those habits become second nature.

Did you know that over 30 percent of all American kids have abnormally high cholesterol levels? That 99 percent of American kids eat sweet desserts at least six times a week? And that, on average, American kids drink twenty-four ounces of soda pop a day? Basically, what's wrong with the diet of our children (and it is drastically and dangerously wrong) is the same thing that's wrong with the diet of American adults:

► We eat too much sugar and salt (much of them coming from soft drinks, snacks, and fast foods).

► Our diets are too heavy in cholesterol and saturated fats (again, from fast foods, lunch meats, fatty red meats, butter, cream, and desserts).

► We don't eat enough of the bran cereals, whole-grain foods, pastas, rice, beans and peas, fresh vegetables and fruits that supply us with fiber and complex carbohydrates.

Eating smart doesn't mean all sprouts and tofu. Good eating can and should also be delicious eating, for kids and adults alike, and kids who are introduced early on to food that is both good-tasting and good for them usually become (and stay) as partial to such food as many other kids do to junk food. Smart eating is also easy to do. Basically, it just means avoiding too much salt, sugar, cholesterol, and saturated fat, eating no more (or less) than what our bodies need to function well, and eating a diet that is balanced daily among the four basic food groups: the high-protein foods, such as meat, fish, poultry, and eggs; dairy products; vegetables and fruits; and grains and cereals (including potatoes, rice, pastas, breads).

Kids also have some special nutritional needs that are specific to certain age groups. Let's look now at a few guidelines that address those needs in infants, toddlers, and preschoolers.

some nutritional guidelines for infants

NOTE: A full treatment of infant nutrition is beyond the scope of this book. For more information than is given here, I recommend the American Academy of Pediatrics' *Caring for Your Baby and Young Child: Birth to Age 5*, edited by Steven Shelov, M.D.; and *Into the Mouths of Babes*, by Susan Tate Firkaly.

beginning solids (four to six months)

Breast milk is nature's best and most complete food for your newborn, and up until about four months old, it (or a formula if you are unable to breastfeed) is all your baby needs. At about four to six months, you will want to start introducing solids. I recommend you introduce solid foods to your baby one at a time and try each for a week to make sure it doesn't cause an allergic reaction. Iron-enriched barley cereal is an excellent solid food to start your baby off with, because it can be mixed with breast milk, water, soy-based formula, or whole cow's milk (ask your pediatrician when to introduce cow's milk; it is usually after about six months), is nonallergenic, easily digested, and provides needed iron. At first, try very small amounts and give your baby only as much as he will gladly accept. Dry cereals that you mix yourself are better than ready-made cereals in a jar, as the ready-made or precooked has less iron and what iron there is is less easily absorbed.

You can also introduce plain yogurt at this time, and babies don't need any sweetener added. (Remember, sugar is one of your child's biggest nutritional enemies later on, and since baby hasn't developed a taste for it yet, why start one now?)

Next, you will do well to introduce vegetables before fruits, as fruits are sweeter and more appealing, and it will be easier to establish the intake of veggies *before* you start something sweet. Sometimes the vegetables' flavor can be strong and even bitter-tasting to the baby, so we recommend starting with the "yellows," such as carrots and sweet potatoes, which are usually more appetizing (and more nutritious) than the "greens," such as green beans or peas.

Probably the best fruit to start your baby off with is either finely mashed banana (thinned with breast milk at first), which you can prepare easily in a baby-food grinder, or unsweetened apple sauce.

Botulism has been caused by feeding uncooked honey to children under twelve months and has led to death in many cases. Do not feed infants honey until after age one.

great solid starts for your baby's diet

cereals: barley, oat, and rice

veggies: avocados, carrots, peas, squash, sweet potatoes

dairy products: yogurt, kefir (both unsweetened), cottage cheese

fruit: apple sauce, bananas, papayas, peaches, pears

meat and poultry: beef, chicken, lamb, turkey

NOTE: Spinach, high in oxalic acid, is not recommended until baby is older.

Eat foods that are closest to their natural form. Cut back on highly processed, canned, frozen, or fast foods.

foods for seven through twelve months

At about seven to eight months, you can start introducing the following foods to your baby's diet: beets, broccoli, bulgur, cabbage, cheese (none that is artificially colored or processed), egg yolk, green beans, peanut butter, potatoes (mashed), spinach, sprouts (ground), squash, tofu, and zucchini. At about nine to ten months, you may begin to include legumes. And at about twelve months, it is fine to introduce your baby to egg white, honey, cow's milk, nuts and seeds, orange juice, and tomatoes. (Don't introduce berries and grapes unless peeled until age two, and when you do, be aware of how well your child chews his food, as berries can cause choking.)

By about seven to eight months, your baby will be getting used to being spoon-fed; and by ten to twelve months, he will be looking for more "finger foods." Good finger foods for babies this age are small pieces of chicken or fish, cereals, well-cooked pastas, well-scrambled eggs, and pieces of banana. Never offer your baby pieces of food that are big or hard enough to choke on. By now your child's eating patterns, the foods you serve, and how those foods are prepared are all well established, and both you and the baby should start enjoying his mealtimes more. At about eight or nine months, start encouraging your baby to feed himself (put an old shower curtain under his chair)—it will be great practice for his hand-eye coordination and hand and finger skills.

Feeding your baby in a relaxed, fun atmosphere, not worrying about where food drops, and being sure that everything offered is fresh, tasty, and nutritious, will get him or her off to a good nutritional start.

Tools and tricks of the trade:

▶ A baby spoon, small plastic plate and/or bowl, and a baby-food grinder are all you will need. It is widely recommended that you grind up foods that are taken from your plate for your baby.

If you begin now to serve foods that you have cooked for yourself, the transition for baby to eating what you eat at the table will be easier later on.

▶ A real time-saver: Make batches of pureed fruits and fruit juices and freeze them (great for teething kids!), then thaw them out two or three at a time for mealtimes.

▶ You can think of your own recipes, but remember to try things like this: if you start your baby on avocado one week, and banana the next, try mixing the two together in the third week—the baby will either find it a real treat or gag on it.

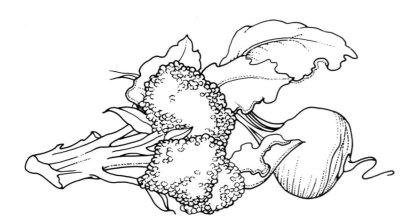

some nutritional guidelines for toddlers and preschoolers

▶ The basic ground rule for feeding your toddler is not to get stuck in a menu rut. Keep things varied and keep his eating interest up with a variety of foods to choose from each week. Toddlers can be *picky* eaters. To avoid turning mealtimes into battlegrounds, offer your child a selection of good, nutritious foods, divided among three small meals and two snacks a day, and let him eat what he wants. If he turns everything down at a particular meal, save the plate for later, when he's hungry. But *don't* allow him to fill up on sweets after refusing to eat a meal.

▶ By your child's first birthday, she should be able to eat most of the foods you eat. Be sure the food you feed her is not too hot and that it is mashed or cut into small enough chunks so that she can't choke on them. Also, food for toddlers shouldn't be heavily sugared, salted, or spiced. At this age, your child needs foods from the same four basic food groups that adults need.

▶ You should avoid adding sugar to your toddler's food and limit his consumption of sweets to an occasional dessert. Snacks should be fruits, vegetables, and cheese and crackers, rather than sweets.

▶ Fats are important to growing children, and I don't recommend that you try to limit your child's consumption of them, including cholesterol, until after two years old—and then only with a gradual cutting back. (I'm assuming here that your child doesn't have a cholesterol or other blood-lipid medical problem.) On the other hand, it *is* a good idea to help your child develop during the toddler years a taste for foods that are low in cholesterol and saturated fats—foods such as fruits, vegetables, chicken, and fish.

finger foods for toddlers:

rice cakes

puffed cereals

crackers

fruit chunks

cheese chunks

pieces of bagels

toast or muffins

vegetable sticks

▶ According to the American Academy of Pediatrics, if your toddler or preschooler is getting a daily diet balanced among the four basic food groups, he probably does not need vitamin supplements. (This is assuming your home is not a vegetarian one; if it is, you should consult your pediatrician as to

which supplements your child might need.) Toddlers and preschoolers do need plenty of calcium for the growth of strong bones and teeth, and it can be had from dairy products such as yogurt, cheese, and milk (a minimum of one to three cups of milk a day is recommended). If your child eats little meat, iron-rich vegetables, or iron-fortified cereal, he *may* need some supplemental iron—ask your pediatrician if you think he might.

▶ By the time your child turns three, mealtime should be family social occasions at which she begins to learn table manners and to participate in the enjoyment of sharing good food. To help your child develop an interest in food and diet, you can begin to let her help in meal planning, shopping, the preparation of meals, table setting, and cleaning up. Talk to your child about why certain foods are good for us and others not so good, and about the relationship between good health and diet.

▶ It is a good idea to start cutting back on high-fat, high-cholesterol foods in your child's diet after about age three. It is recommended that you go to 2 percent milk, low-fat cheeses and yogurt; use margarine instead of butter; and begin to favor fish and chicken over red meat in your family meals. You should also continue to limit your child's intake of sweets. TV, with all its ads for sugary foods, is no help in this effort—which is another good reason to limit television time. Also, you should avoid overfeeding your preschooler, as it may lead to overweight and/or obesity later on. Remember, the eating habits he is developing now will very likely be with him for the rest of his life!

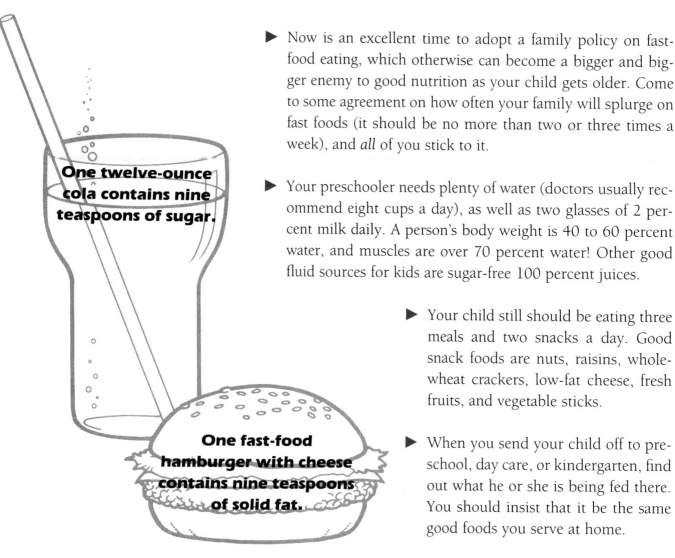

One twelve-ounce cola contains nine teaspoons of sugar.

One fast-food hamburger with cheese contains nine teaspoons of solid fat.

▶ Now is an excellent time to adopt a family policy on fast-food eating, which otherwise can become a bigger and bigger enemy to good nutrition as your child gets older. Come to some agreement on how often your family will splurge on fast foods (it should be no more than two or three times a week), and *all* of you stick to it.

▶ Your preschooler needs plenty of water (doctors usually recommend eight cups a day), as well as two glasses of 2 percent milk daily. A person's body weight is 40 to 60 percent water, and muscles are over 70 percent water! Other good fluid sources for kids are sugar-free 100 percent juices.

▶ Your child still should be eating three meals and two snacks a day. Good snack foods are nuts, raisins, whole-wheat crackers, low-fat cheese, fresh fruits, and vegetable sticks.

▶ When you send your child off to preschool, day care, or kindergarten, find out what he or she is being fed there. You should insist that it be the same good foods you serve at home.

arnold's smart eating tips for your entire family

Here are some good basic nutritional habits (some of them taken or adapted from Dr. Kenneth Cooper's "Positive Eating Plan") that your whole family should try to develop. You'll be surprised at how easy it is to incorporate these habits into your family life; and remember, *you* are your child's best role model for all fitness practices, including good nutrition.

▶ Establish consistent eating patterns for your family, including three meals a day.

▶ Eat a balanced diet—with a variety of foods at each meal—that includes 50 percent carbohydrates, 20 percent protein, and 30 percent fat.

▶ Don't eat more than you need—push away from the table *before* you are full.

▶ Prepare foods in ways that minimize the use of fat (for example, steaming veggies instead of frying them in butter or lard; broiling, baking, or grilling chicken, meat, and fish rather than frying them; and using Pam when you do fry).

▶ Leave skins on your vegetables and potatoes whenever possible.

▶ Shop for fresh produce—right from the garden or the farmers' market is best (the grocer's produce section is second-best; frozen or low-salt canned is next best).

▶ Eat only low-calorie, low-salt, low-sugar, and low-fat snacks.

▶ Eat slowly, chew your food well, and only *eat* while you're eating—no TV or reading. Also, eat sitting at a table, not standing, walking around, or driving. Toddlers should *always* be seated and watched while eating.

▶ Don't keep foods in the house that you don't want your kids to eat. Keep plenty of the foods you *want* them to eat and make them easily available, like fruit in a basket.

▶ Try to eat dinner together as a family at least five nights a week.

▶ Breakfast, particularly for kids, is the most important meal of the day. *Never* let your kids skip or skimp on breakfast. If you have to skip a meal, let it be lunch.

▶ Help your child acquire a taste for new foods that are healthful and nutritious, such as asparagus, yams, watercress, and kiwifruit. The wider your child's taste in foods, the easier and more fun smart eating becomes. But also remember, you will never help a child to like a particular food by forcing him to eat it.

▶ There are plenty of good books on how and why to eat smart. Get one or two and read them.

▶ Eating, like exercise, is one of life's great pleasures. Do it smart, but *enjoy* it, and teach your kids to enjoy it.

when arnold was young

My best friend while growing up was Sigmund Volroyd. He lived on the farm next to our house, and Meinhard and I helped Sigmund and his older brother Franz with their chores. We did things like cut hay and milk cows and clean stalls. Working with animals and farm equipment was fun and we were always eager to help. And by helping our friends do their chores, all of us could get away sooner to do kid things, like sledding in winter and swimming in summer.

There was a two-room schoolhouse in Thal that was very old and had a wooden floor with holes in it. It was an elementary school for thirty children between the ages of five and ten. Our teacher's name was Mr. Bochman. He divided the room and the class into two grades. First-graders were five, six, and seven years old, second-graders were eight and nine. First grade sat on the left side of the room, second grade sat on the right side. At the front of the room, behind the teacher's desk, was a big blackboard. Mr. Bochman drew a line down the middle of it with white chalk and then wrote each grade's lessons on the side facing the students in that half of the room. Mr. Bochman would give a reading or writing assignment to one grade and then teach the other. After a while he would switch sides, so that each grade was taught for the same amount of time.

Mr. Bochman was a very serious teacher who made certain his students learned their lessons. He was very strict and did not tolerate any whispering or staring out of windows. Because he was so strict with us, Mr. Bochman allowed us outside for ten minutes every hour. This was so we could release some of the energy that had been building up inside us while in the classroom. Outside we played tag or soccer or handball. And sometimes after a rain, Mr. Bochman would take the entire class on a mushroom hunt in the near woods. Off we would go to collect mushrooms for our mothers, who would use them in soups and sauces.

when arnold was young

The school was two miles from our house, and Meinhard and I walked there every morning with our friends. On the way we would kick a soccer ball back and forth to one another and have contests to see who could kick it the farthest. Sigmund and Franz and Meinhard could kick the ball farther than I could. Something deep inside me didn't like losing all the time, so I practiced kicking the ball after school. One day a girl named Annaliese watched me practicing and said I was doing it wrong. She told me her two older brothers played on the national soccer team and that they had taught her how to kick and pass and dribble a soccer ball. At first I didn't want a girl to teach me. But after I saw how good she was, I agreed. And one day I beat everyone in the neighborhood and kicked the ball all the way over farmer Kruck's hay field. Annaliese taught me a valuable lesson, one that I've always remembered. Never be afraid to ask someone for help.

When I was ten years old, I attended junior high school in Graz, a city that is five miles from Thal. In order to do my chores and meet the school bus that took students to Graz, I had to wake up at six A.M. I would dress and wash and brush my teeth and then get fresh milk for my mother from the Volroyds. Then Meinhard and I would bring in water and wood. In winter we would also shovel snow from the paths that led to the well and the road. For breakfast my mother would make hot chocolate and porridge, which was made from cornmeal and called polenta. Sometimes she would put powdered sugar on top of the porridge and it would taste warm and sweet. Other times she would add bits of bacon to it and it would taste crunchy. While Meinhard and I ate breakfast, my mother would pack our lunch. She always included raw carrots and celery, a piece of fruit, and small loaves of bread that had delicious fruit fillings.

In junior high school I participated in gymnastics and running and jumping events. And Sigmund and I played on our school soccer team three days a week. After school all the children in my neighborhood would gather in the field across from our house and play different sports. We even had neighborhood championships in badminton and volleyball. In the fall my father would leave work early and meet us after school for soccer practice. Sometimes he would coach us and other times he would play with us because he liked to exercise. When our village soccer team played other village teams, my father was often asked to referee the game, because he was a policeman and considered a very honest man.

PROGRAMS

3 outside the home

Preparing a child for a life of fitness and good health begins, as we have seen, in the home. In order to provide your child with the best possible head start toward lifetime fitness, physical activity, love of movement, and good nutrition should be normal and necessary aspects of the family environment he or she is born into and grows up in. Nothing can substitute for the home in providing that head start for preschool children, or in maintaining it with family fitness activity at least into adolescence (see *Arnold's Fitness for Kids Ages 6–10*), but in some cases preschool exercise programs outside the home can be very helpful in supplementing that head start.

In this chapter, I will discuss the pros and cons of such programs and describe some of the best of them for you. I will also outline for you what you should expect from kindergarten physical education for your five-year-old. Then I'll give you a list of national fitness programs available to kindergartens, and a list of preschool exercise/play videotapes and records that you can use in your home or recommend for use to your child's nursery school, day-care center, or kindergarten. And finally, we'll take a look toward your child's future involvement in organized sports.

Organized play and exercise programs for preschoolers seem to be sprouting up all over the country recently, and experts are divided as to their value. A two-year study by the American Academy of Pediatrics found that such programs do not advance kids physically. Some authorities believe that they are simply unnecessary, since preschoolers get enough exercise naturally, and others believe that overly structured and/or highly competitive programs can actually be emotionally and physically dangerous to children. That is very likely true, and parents should be warned of that possibility, but it shouldn't keep you from looking into one or more well-regarded preschool fitness programs or from entering your child in one of them if you like what you find. And while it is also true that most preschoolers can naturally get all the exercise they need, they can do so only if they are provided with plenty of space and supervision. These programs can be great if you don't have a backyard or an extra room in your house to turn into a play area, or if you can't resist the temptation whenever you have some free time to pop the tot in the playpen, grab a pint of ice cream, and park yourself in front of the tube.

In fact, the very best thing about preschooler exercise programs is that the great majority of them involve you and your child *together* and therefore increase the amount of time you spend with each other. Other pluses to preschooler exercise programs are:

▶ You will get to know other parents who care about their children's health, and you will pick up lots of new play and exercise options to add to your family play sessions.

▶ Your child will probably enjoy playing on a regular basis with other kids (as well as with you), and will get an introduction to interaction with other kids, listening skills, and functioning as part of a group that will help prepare him for kindergarten. The programs are also helpful in preparing kids for the physical education and sports programs they will enter in school.

▶ The good programs are imaginative, entertaining, and *fun* for kids (and probably will be for you too), and, early in a child's life, put exercise in the context of pleasure and enjoyment.

If you think a preschool exercise program might be right for you and your child, I recommend you go together and try out a few before settling on the best one for you. Here are a few things to look for:

▶ First of all, your child should enjoy the program and *want* to go to it. *Don't* force him or her into one of these programs.

▶ Unless you are just looking for an active form of baby-sitting, the program should involve one or both parents.

▶ It should have a trained instructor, and one whom you and your child like.

▶ It should offer developmentally and age-appropriate equipment and activities. Kids who crawl should be together, doing things that are appropriate for crawlers, not toddlers. Make sure the program presents activities and opportunities that *your* child is developmentally ready to succeed at and enjoy.

▶ It should be imaginative, never boring, and should use various colors and shapes and music to excite and motivate kids to enjoy moving. You will quickly be able to tell if the routines are well paced and innovative—just look at your child. Is she having fun?

Finally, once you have chosen a program, your child may or may not jump right into it immediately. If she is a little shy at first—even after two or three sessions—don't worry about it and don't push her to join in before she wants to. Kids learn a lot just by sitting and watching, and she'll start participating when she's ready.

some preschooler exercise programs you might want to look into

Most YMCAs around the country—as well as many YWCAs, YW-YMHAs, and some city departments of parks and recreation—offer preschooler exercise programs, some for kids as young as three or four months old. Here is a typical, small-city YMCA offering of classes, these under a preschooler exercise program called "Healthy Start."

parent/tot: 13 through 24 months old

parent/child: 25 through 35 months old

tiny tots: 3 to 4½ years old

kindergarten: 4½ to 6 years old

Healthy Start focuses on the physical and social development of kids by providing games, activities, songs, and movement that are age-appropriate. Parents are involved throughout and are also counseled on safety and nutrition. This same YMCA offers a similar preschooler aquatics program, and a youth sports skills development program for kids three through six and their parents, which teaches soccer and basketball skills in a "cooperative setting of fun and bonding between parent and child."

There are several nationally franchised preschooler exercise programs that are available in many communities throughout the country. Gymboree and Playorena are two programs that offer forty-five-minute classes held once a week for kids and parents together and are taught by well-trained instructors. Both stress bonding between parent and child, semistructured play, and the use of music and colorful play equipment to keep kids entertained and having fun.

Gymboree offers the following classes: *Cradlegym* (newborns to three months old) supplies parents of newborns with support and a chance to share their experiences, while the babies enjoy the sensory stimulation of music, movement, and gentle songs. *Babygym* (three to twelve months) provides an atmosphere where infants can socialize with other babies their age. It uses specially built play equipment, and introduces bright-colored objects and rhythmic songs. Parents are given a printed parent's guide outlining ideas and items that can be used in the home to create a similar experience. *Gymboree I* (ten to sixteen months) is designed for almost/just walkers with games and activities in a noncompetitive setting that makes walking more fun than ever! *Gymboree II* (twelve to thirty months) is for the walking-running-talking children of this age group, and caters to their urges to explore and to their growing imaginations (theme days are held like "Wild West Day" and "Under and Through"), and uses equipment built just for them that they can roll on, swing on, and jump on to their hearts' content. *Gymboree III* (two-year-olds) encourages children to sing their own songs during "Parachute and Circle" times, and provides them with a more active role in rhythmic movements and play. Finally, *Gymgrad* (two and a half to four years) begins to get children ready for sports with noncompetitive gymnastics such as tumbling, games with special props, and "Gymbercises" for kids and parents, which develop coordination and overall body strength.

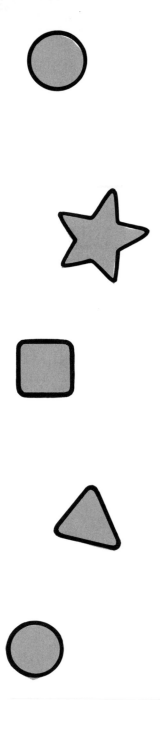

Playorena's classes are also divided up by age groups (somewhat loosely to allow for developmental differences). *Hello World* (three through eleven months): precrawlers and crawlers delight in bright colors and shapes while enjoying gentle exercises done to soothing music and songs. *First Steps* (nine through seventeen months): colorful play equipment provides lots of safe, soft motivation for the beginning walker to stand up and take a step or two. *Toddlers* (thirteen through twenty-four months): kids practice balance, going uphill and downhill, rocking, bouncing, and participating in group activities. *Runners* (eighteen to thirty-six months): children climb, jump, run, and dance during songs, activities, and games. *Jumpers* (thirty to forty-seven months): older children with higher levels of interest and attention participate in a variety of skill-building play activities.

These are the qualities I like about Gymboree and Playorena. I suggest you check out your local programs to make sure they offer these same features.

An excellent model preschooler exercise program that puts more emphasis on skills development than most is the RightStart program offered by the Children's Hospital of Illinois at Saint Francis Medical Center in Peoria, Illinois. This innovative program is a parent *and* child program that offers eight-week sessions for children ages eighteen months through five years. There are two certified instructors per class. The classes meet once a week for forty-five minutes to one hour, with limited class size. Instructors start with a warm-up to enhance

sociability as well as movement, and for the three- to five-year-old, the program may include movement themes such as body-part identification, locomotor movements, directions, levels, spatial awareness, shapes, etc. The parent and child then proceed to rotate through eighteen to twenty different skills "stations" while instructors assist. The use of developmentally appropriate equipment is emphasized in this program to enhance skills as well as insure success in this non-competitive approach to learning and practicing correct pattern development of skills. Instructional skill areas include throwing, kicking, striking, catching, jumping, balance, spatial awareness, and fitness activities. Kids get to "play" with their parents, while the parents and instructors provide the teaching component. Parents are involved throughout in the evaluation, implementation, and supervision of the child's learning experience. Prior to the three- to five-year-old program, the parents attend a special class on the pattern development of skills in early childhood. Teaching and learning do not stop after class, since parents have learned about skills development, worked with their children and the instructors, and thus know how to continue to encourage and teach these skills outside the class. If you would like more information on this program, you may contact Suzi Boos or Mary Jo Jones at the Children's Hospital of Illinois at Saint Francis Medical Center, 530 NE Glen Oak Avenue, Peoria, IL 61637, telephone (309) 655-7171.

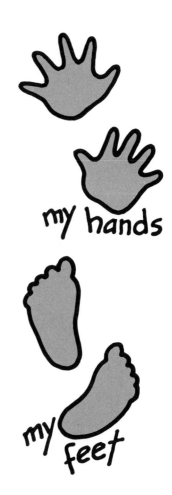

my hands

my feet

Another innovative and exciting program that can be emulated in your home, or in your community if you live in a place that doesn't offer any kind of exercise class for preschoolers, is Kids' Aerobics, developed and taught by Becky Davang at the Sugar Land Athletic Club in Sugar Land, Texas. Ms. Davang holds once-a-week, forty-five-minute classes for three- through seven-year-olds that give kids cardiovascular exercise as well as stretching and skills practice—all of it packaged colorfully and imaginatively. Kids simply love this program. Each class is broken into five phases. In Phase I, the kids warm up and stretch by raising their arms over their heads to "push the ceiling up" or by lowering their arms to "push the floor back to the ground." Arms become tree branches, fingers become leaves, abdominals are stretched to "look for worms," and "frog races" stretch the hamstrings. In Phase II, the "Move It" phase, the kids' heart rates are increased by "marching in a parade," "tiptoeing like mice," "galloping like horses," "hopping like bunnies," etc. Phase III is balance and coordination play. Kids go through an obstacle course of body rolls, somersaults, walking the balance beam, crawling through a tunnel, jumping on a mini-trampoline, running through a hopscotch of Hula Hoops; they end their third circuit of the course by catching a ball and throwing it back through a Hula Hoop. Phase IV, "Rhythm and Movement," begins lowering the children's heart rates by having them play with props, such as three-foot-long streamers cut from an old sheet, and having them shake potato chip cans filled with popcorn kernels and wrapped in duct tape. In the final "Cool-Down Phase," there is more stretching, a story, and drumming on empty coffee cans wrapped in tape. Ms. Davang ends her class with the kids holding hands in a big circle and saying loudly, "Exercise makes smart brains, strong muscles, and strong hearts!"

For more information on Kids' Aerobics, write Becky Davang, 12322 Tambourine, Stafford, TX 77477.

kindergarten

Like preschooler exercise classes, a good kindergarten physical education program can supplement (but by no means replace) your efforts in the home to provide your child with a good head start on lifetime fitness and good health.

Not all kindergartens offer physical education classes, and in some of the ones that do, "PE" is really just an unorganized recess or play period. Personally, I believe that *all* kindergartens should be required by state law to offer quality daily physical education taught by physical education specialists, and as chairman of the President's Council on Physical Fitness and Sports, I am working hard to make that happen. In the meantime, if your child goes to kindergarten, you owe it to him or her and to yourself to find out what, if any, physical education is offered there. If none is offered, you can just accept that and keep up religiously with your play period schedule at home, or you can work (by yourself or with other parents who care about their kids' good health) to get a good physical education program initiated at your child's kindergarten.

To do that—or to try to improve an already existing program—you should know what constitutes an ideal kindergarten physical education program. Here are a few guidelines:

► Physical education classes should be held daily (three times a week minimum) for twenty-five to thirty-five minutes.

► Classes should be taught by physical education specialists.

► There should be enough facilities and equipment for every student in the class.

► Classes should be no larger than fifteen to twenty kids per instructor.

► Physical education opportunities should be equal for boys and girls.

► Classes should incorporate instruction in movement and listening skills, rule-following and group behavior, stretching, and some vigorous aerobic activities, all within a pressure-free, noncompetitive environment of fun and play.

There are a number of excellent exercise and/or fitness testing programs for kids that have been developed over the past ten to fifteen years specifically for schools and kindergartens to put into place or to use to supplement existing programs. I am listing two of those here so that you, as a parent, can, if need be, let your child's kindergarten or school know they exist, and also for the sake of any PE teacher who might read this book and who feels the need for a little help with his or her program. Also perhaps helpful to the kindergarten physical education teacher, as well as to parents who might want to use them in the home, are a number of very good records and audio and visual tapes of preschool exercise and play. Those are also listed below.

The President's National Youth Fitness Program. A cooperative effort of AAHPERD and the President's Council on Physical Fitness and Sports, this new program is modeled on AAHPERD's Physical Best and the President's Council's President's Challenge.* For more information, please contact AAHPERD or The President's Council on Physical Fitness and Sports, 701 Pennsylvania Avenue, NW, Washington, DC 20004, telephone (202) 272-3421.

American Alliance of Health, Physical Education, Recreation and Dance (AAHPERD), 1900 Association Drive, Reston, VA 22091, telephone (703) 476-3400. AAHPERD's Physical Best program is a comprehensive physical fitness education and assessment program designed to motivate all children and youth to participate in physical activity to develop their *personal best*. Physical Best can help teachers and parents change the way children think about their own physical fitness. This program is the first to combine assessment of health-related fitness with practical classroom instructional materials that teach why and how to stay fit for a lifetime. (Grades K through 12.)

* A fitness test for children ages six to seventeen.

preschooler exercise tapes for use in kindergarten or home

"Moving and Learning for Early Elementary"—a set of audiotapes produced by Human Kinetics and authored by Rae Pica. List price: $19.90 per cassette, or $140.00 for set of six.

"Kids in Motion"—an imaginative video filled with music, dancing, and exercise, developed by Julie Weissman. List price: $19.98.

a word toward the future

By the time your child turns five, organized team sports programs are right around the corner. Let's look for a moment at what your concerns about those programs should be.

Few experiences in a child's life *can* be as rewarding, as much fun, as educational, and as character-building as participation in team sports. At their best, sports teach cooperation, discipline, self-control, timing, how to set and realize goals, and other worthy lessons. They can build egos, and they can create in a child a deep self-confidence that carries over into other things the child does. And finally, learning early to enjoy sports can have the best possible influence on the development of your child's life-fitness habits by sugarcoating the pill of exercise. On the other side of this coin, few experiences in a child's life can be as damaging as a bad experience with team sports—as destructive of confidence, as tough on the ego and self-esteem, as unrewarding, as un-fun. And such an experience can be, and often is, the *worst* possible influence on the development of good fitness habits by turning a child off exercise and physical activity, sometimes for life.

And who determines which kind of experience your child will have with team sports? It could be a school physical education teacher, a Little League coach, even other children. But if you are smart, it will be you, and only you. Just as *you* must control your child's physical development and education in the home, so must you take the ultimate responsibility for guiding your child toward the *right* kind of team sports participation—either at school or in the community—and away from the wrong kind. What are the right and wrong kinds of team sports participation for young children? Here are a few guidelines:

▶ Never push your child into any sport solely because *you* want him or her to play it. ("Little Tommy's going to be an ace shortstop just like his dad was.") Talk over the pros and cons of various sports, team and individual, with your child and let him or her decide which, if any, to take up. Ideally, kids should begin with one or more of the "individual," life-fitness sports, like swimming or biking, and then move on to team sports.

▶ Don't let your child enter into a sport before he or she is developmentally ready to play and enjoy it. Kids develop emotionally and physically at different speeds. If your five-year-old boy, for example, is a little slow developing eye-foot coordination and agility, and has a hard time concentrating on plays and game strategies, he is probably not ready to begin playing organized soccer.

▶ A sport, like fitness, *has to be fun in order for a kid to stick with it.* Encourage your child to try out as many team and individual sports as possible, looking for the ones he or she has fun playing.

▶ Any school or community sports program that emphasizes winning over fun, over general participation (by *every* kid who wants to be on the team), and over good sportsmanship, should be avoided like the plague. There is plenty of time for your child to get really skilled at a sport and to become an intense competitor, if that is going to happen. Between ages five and ten, he or she should enjoy, participate, and improve at his or her own speed, and learn how to win and lose fairly, generously, and gracefully.

▶ Also avoid programs that have too much adult interference in them, from either over-zealous coaches or parents. Sports should belong to the kids at this age. Whatever coaching your child *is* receiving should be skilled and knowledgeable.

▶ Both gymnastics and soccer are excellent sports for young kids to start with, as both help develop a variety of movement skills.

▶ According to Thomas Fahey, author of *Competitive Sports and Your Child,* "Five- to ten-year-olds should belong to organized teams only if those teams provide an atmosphere for learning a variety of movement fundamentals and for developing a love of the sport."

That sums it up pretty well.

Finally, though the right kinds of organized team sports can play a valuable role in your child's development and contribute significantly to the laying of a good life-fitness foundation during ages five through ten, they are certainly not necessary to either that development or that foundation. If your child doesn't want to play team sports, or plays one for a while and drops out, fine. Play golf with him; introduce her to tennis; take a karate or aquatics class or dance class together, or go cross-country skiing. If *your* attitude toward sports is that they are, above all else, enjoyable corollaries to a healthy, energetic, fun life, then that attitude will rub off and your child will find the individual sports that he or she can employ in that way.

when arnold was young

When my father was a young man, he was a very good athlete and competed in swimming and gymnastics and many other sports. He even worked out with weights and dumbbells that he made himself from discarded steel and iron. But the sport he liked best was ice curling. He competed in the Austrian and European championships and trained for them every winter on the lake that was close to our house. There were two competitions in ice curling, one for distance and one for accuracy. My father liked competing in the distance event. In fact, my earliest memory is of being on the lake with my father and brother when he was practicing throwing the fifteen-pound wooden "stone" down the ice. It was Meinhard's and my job to help make an alley on the ice for my father to practice on. The alley had to be four hundred feet long and ten feet wide. After it was shoveled and swept, my father would throw two stones down the ice, and Meinhard and I would chase after them until they stopped. Then we would have our own contest to see who could push them back to our father the fastest. It was my first competition and my first lesson in the importance of hard work and practice.

My family participated in other outdoor activities, too. My mother and father enjoyed hiking, bicycling, and sledding, and they taught us to enjoy

them. We took long hikes into the forests and mountains in summer, and we went sledding in winter. There were no mountains for skiing close to our home, just rolling hills that were perfect for sledding. We didn't own bicycles of our own, but sometimes my father would borrow a few from the police station and we would take bike rides and have picnics. And on weekends my family would take walks to other villages and visit with friends and relatives.

APPENDIX

play exercises for kids
from birth through age five

part I: birth to one year
part II: one year to three years
part III: three years to six years

▶ A note about performing these play exercises with your child: never force your child to do any of these activities. It is important to take your cues *from* the child and to understand that if the child is not ready to do a certain play exercise, it is always best to wait for another time, when he or she is eager to do it. Infants, toddlers, and preschoolers all naturally love movement and play/interaction *with the parent,* so you will probably have no trouble engaging your child's interest in any of these activities. But remember: a forced activity will remain in your child's memory as a negative experience, thus creating a negative reaction to any future type of movement. Keep it light, easy and relaxed, and most of all—FUN!

▶ Each of the "General Play" sections that follow for the infant should be allowed as much of the day as possible (that is, when baby is not being fed, napping, having a bath, being changed, or doing some of the other play exercises with you!). As simple as they are, they are very important to young minds and bodies that are learning and growing. Independent baby play (self-teaching) is definitely "baby's work."

▶ Don't limit yourself just to the play exercises given here. This is not intended to be a comprehensive list, merely examples of the *sorts* of activities you can do with your child to start building a good foundation for fitness. Use your imagination and knowledge of your child to come up with other developmentally appropriate and fun play exercises.

▶ Physically active games, such as different variations of tag, keep-away, and Simon Says, are excellent to spice up play periods with four- and five-year-olds.

▶ Some five- and even four-year-olds may be ready to take up one of the "lifetime sports," such as cross-country or downhill skiing, swimming, or even one of the martial arts. You should be confident that the child really *wants* to take up the sport and is developmentally ready to do so before letting him enter a program, and then you should make certain that he is being taught the sport by someone trained to teach it to small children.

▶ Remember, don't push your child any further or faster than he or she wants to go. Children all develop at different speeds. Your job is to determine what your child can do and enjoys doing at a particular stage of development and then to join him in play that encourages those activities and helps develop the motor skills that underlie them.

part I: birth to one year

birth to three months

1. Arm Stretch Let baby grip your fingers with his hands while he is lying on his back, then gently spread his arms up over his head and down toward his hips, then spread his arms out toward his sides and back in toward his chest until his wrists cross. Now repeat the whole sequence, slowly and gently, two or three times at first, working up to eight times total. This will exercise the muscles and joints of the arms, shoulders, and chest.

2. Leg Stretch Again, with baby lying on the floor facing you (you can do this on the changing table too), gently grasp both ankles in your hands and push slowly upward until baby's knees are raised to the tummy; hold only for a moment, then release and allow baby's legs to completely straighten. Repeat this five times, working up to as many as baby wants to do.

3. Eye Stretch With baby lying on his back or in a bouncer, use a toy or object that is bright and colored either black and white or in primary colors (something flashy that stands out against its background), and attract your baby's attention with it. Once you have his attention, have him follow the object with his eyes as you slowly move it back and forth in front of him (at birth, babies can see objects eight to ten inches from them very well, so start there). You should do this only for a short time at first, say two to three minutes, then gradually work up to five to eight minutes. Use different objects so baby doesn't get bored, and engage in chatter with your baby at the same time. This will accustom the baby to tracking a moving object.

4. General Play On tummy: place baby on his or her tummy on the floor with a few stimulating toys (black and white or primary colors are usually most attractive) for baby to reach out and grasp. Toys should be those that either make a noise when shaken or squeak when squeezed, and can be put in the mouth. The baby's entire body is exercised here as he or she reaches, stretches, grasps, and tries to scoot around to get various toys. This type of play will be most fun for the baby who can hold his head up off the floor. If he can't, place the toys in visual range of where he *is* looking while lying on his tummy.

On back: place baby flat on her back in crib or playpen with some toys hung in front of her so that she can (1) see the toys and (2) reach and grasp for them. Whatever you use to hang the toys, be sure it can't break or be swallowed and be sure it's not so long that the baby can get caught in it.

three to six months

NOTE: In addition to these activities, at about three or four months, your baby will be ready to be put into a Jolly Jumper, which hangs in a doorway or archway and is used for the baby to swing, dangle, and bounce. This product is great for allowing your baby to build muscles in his legs, and to get him accustomed to vertical movement. (Important: baby should be able to hold his head and shoulders steady before he is ready for this jumper.)

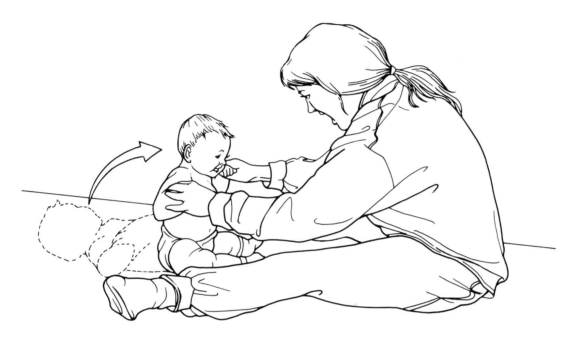

1. Pull-Ups With baby lying on his back in front of you, allow him to grasp your fingers with his hands and then gently pull the baby up, at first only a little bit, then all the way up to a sitting position. (Depending on your baby's development, you may begin this exercise sooner than three months.) Do this two or three times at first, working up to as many as baby wants to do. You will be able to sense fatigue or boredom.

2. Cyclegs Use the same position as for the Leg Stretch in the "Birth to Three Month" section, but this time alternate moving the baby's legs up and down as though he were riding a bicycle.

3. Superbaby Holding your baby securely around the torso, lift her overhead (or over your body if you are lying down) and let her "fly." This increases baby's spatial awareness, allows for total body movement—and babies love it.

4. General Play Baby will probably be able to sit by herself by five to six months, so you can arrange her toys around her on the floor, sit down and play with her, pausing occasionally to observe how she plays with the toys. You can hand toys to her, and take them back if she wants to give them to you. She is working on playing with her own hands by touching them together, picking things up, putting them down, passing them from hand to hand, getting them into and out of her mouth, shaking them, and stretching for out-of-reach objects. She will probably use a raking motion at first to get toys to her, and then refine this motion, eventually being able to pick up small objects on the first try. All of this play is very important developmentally, improving hand-eye coordination and hand and finger skills. Try rolling a ball toward her and across the floor in front of her to encourage her visual tracking and convergence skills.

six to nine months

1. Standing Ovation Seat the baby in your lap; baby is supported under the arms as he stands up, squats back down, and stands again. This kind of play is excellent for building leg muscles and developing coordination and balance. Eventually, baby will start to "walk up" the front of Mom's or Dad's body.

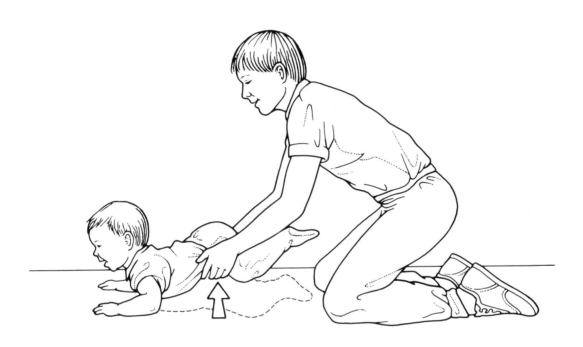

2. Wheelbarrow (stationary) This exercise will be modified as baby gets older, but for now, place baby on his tummy with elbows resting on the floor supporting his upper body. Now firmly grasp baby's tummy/pelvis area and lift. Hold for three to five seconds at first. Most babies love this new sensation. You can increase the length of time you hold the baby—up to seven to ten seconds—and do it as many times as the baby enjoys it.

3. General Play Your baby probably will have begun crawling around by now and will be very interested in anything out of reach. Rather than frustrate him during play, make sure everything he *can* get to (in at least one room in your house) is something he is allowed to play with. You can even make a game of lining up some interesting toys and stuffed animals on the lower levels of coffee tables and end tables and under chairs. In our family room, we have a TV stand with drawers in the bottom (with all valuables now removed and stored elsewhere) that contain hidden treasures. Before play begins, we put a few favorite toys in the drawers and watch the wonder and surprise when our daughter discovers them there!

Since baby is getting around more now, rather than limit his movement, make sure there is at least one room that is safe for him to play and roam in. *Roaming is most of what he'll want to do, and it is very good exercise for him.* He will also sit and closely examine his toys, showing particular interest in buttons, strings, and the sounds things make. At about seven to nine months, he will begin to pull himself up on furniture or your pantleg, and start to "cruise" around the house holding on to furniture. At this point, you can place toys around on tops of chairs and tables, which will further entice your child to get from one place to another to "retrieve" a favorite friend. Encourage your baby to use his fingers and hands in as many fun ways as possible, and continue rolling balls to him and in front of him at various speeds.

nine to twelve months

1. Superbaby II Same as Superbaby, except this time the parent places the soles of his feet under baby's tummy and, holding on to baby's arms, raises baby up in the air. Parent can raise and lower baby by bending knees. This provides more opportunity for space and movement exploration.

2. Wheelbarrow II (nonstationary) Same as Wheelbarrow, but instead of staying still, baby can walk forward on his hands while his pelvis is being held up in the air.

3. Blanket Trick Use one of baby's blankets for this: allow baby to grasp the blanket firmly with both hands while on his tummy, then slowly and carefully drag the blanket toward you. At first baby may let go abruptly, but after a while he will understand it's fun and hang on for the ride.

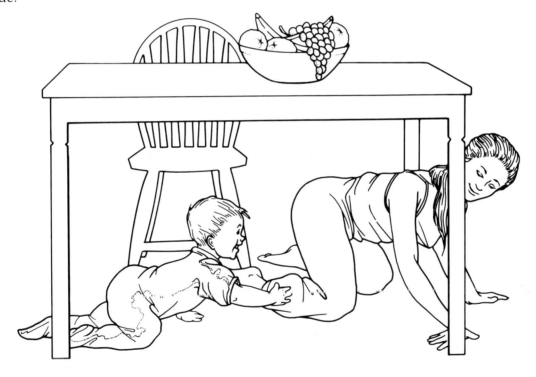

4. In and Out Chairs are cleared away from kitchen or dining room table. Parent crawls under table on all fours and then back out, and encourages child to follow. Parent can follow child as well. Child can learn *in* and *out*. Also, crawl around a leg of the table, or around the whole table, and child learns *around*. This is good for learning how to follow direction after demonstration.

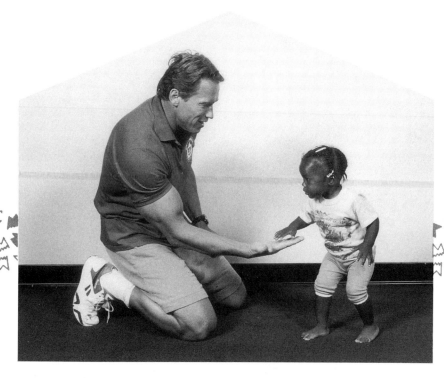

5. Walkin' Fool Your baby will be ready to walk somewhere in this age range, and will need some help to establish confidence at first. It's best to offer support by holding baby around the torso, under the arms, rather than holding on to a hand. In this way, baby learns earlier how to balance and doesn't feel as though he's relying on holding someone's hand in order to walk. In the beginning, parents can kneel on the floor facing each other with baby taking tentative steps back and forth between the two. Eventually, baby will take off on his own, never looking back!

part II: one year to three years

In this section, there will be some play exercises that work on movement, some on strength, and some on skills development—many include elements of all three. Experts believe that most fine-motor-skills development is firmly established between the ages of one and three. So it is very important to encourage as much hand and finger movement as possible during your child's second and third years.

one to two years

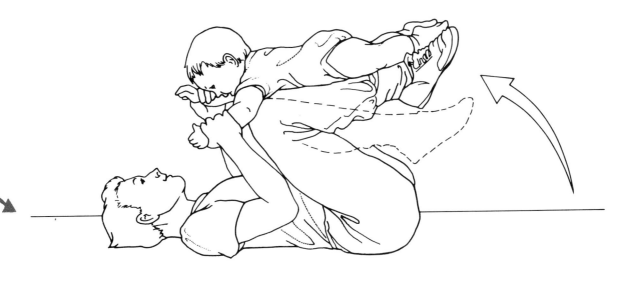

1. Shin-Tow Parent lies on his back with legs together and knees bent and places the baby on his shins so that he is facing parent as parent holds firmly on to forearms. Parents lifts baby into the air on his shins and bounces gently, then lowers back down. This can be done as many times as the child likes. This play/exercise is great for increasing your toddler's love of movement; and all the while, parent explains what *up* and *down* mean.

2. Stretch High and Reach Low Parent gets on his knees (so he doesn't tower over toddler); parent and child face each other and both raise their arms into the air, stretching hands and fingers toward the sky. They can pretend to be tree branches reaching for the clouds, saying "Rain on me—I need to grow!" or reaching for the sun, saying "Shine on me—I need to grow!" Then they both lower their arms down to the ground, reaching low to look for seeds (like a bird) or to look for water with their trunks (like an elephant).

3. Follow the Mommy (or Follow the Daddy, or Grandpa, etc.) Walkers love to follow you around, so rather than feel like you're being followed, turn it into a game! Go around the kitchen table two or three times, slowly enough so that baby can keep up a few steps behind, then head off in another direction, into the family room, circle once around, and back into the kitchen. Do this for ten to fifteen minutes and child will get plenty of exercise as you play Follow the Leader. You can do this to music, and even start marching as you go! Have a parade and have the dog and cat join in!

4. On a Roll Parent and child sit on the floor with legs spread, feet touching and facing each other. Using a volleyball-size ball, roll the ball to the child and ask him or her to roll it back to you. Clap your hands when the child catches the ball. Eventually, you may move farther apart and try rolling from a greater distance. The point here is to learn how to catch with both hands and how to roll toward a large target.

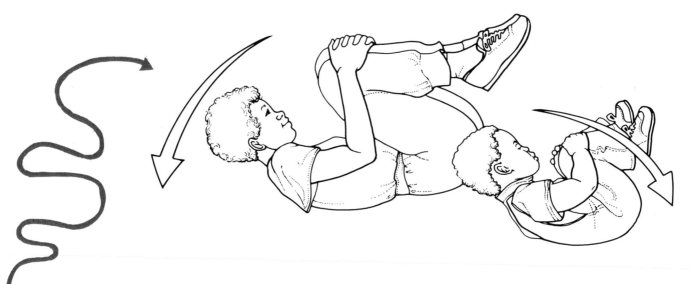

5. Rockin' Robin Parent and child both lie on the floor side by side with arms holding knees to chest and head tucked in toward chest. Now both rock slowly back and forth from top of shoulders to buttocks. This exercise stretches the hamstring and shoulder/arm muscles and mildly strengthens the abdominal muscles.

6. Foot Toss Child and parent lie on the floor or ground with legs outstretched in front of them. One of the two has a volleyball-size ball held between the ankles, and lifts the ball off the floor and thrusts it into the air, releasing it. Then the other person does the same thing. The object is to try and get the ball high into the air.

two to three years

NOTE: For this age child, the more running, piggybacking, rolling, climbing, and sliding, etc., that you can get into his play, the better. Also, continue to encourage hand and finger skills: building block towers, turning handles, drawing, scribbling, screwing and unscrewing jars—all are good practice. Make a "balance beam" by laying a sanded two-by-four board on the ground, and practice different movements on it.

1. Bouncy Ball Parent and child stand facing each another, about four to five feet apart at first, and bounce a volleyball-size ball back and forth to each other. The two can begin to move farther apart after this exercise becomes easy for the child. Bounce as many times as child wants to.

2. Volleyball Stretch (standing) Same as above, except standing and using volleyball-size ball. This works the hamstring and calf muscles more.

3. Stick Hop Parent holds broomstick or mop out about four or five inches off the floor or ground and child is encouraged to step over it, or hop or skip over it. This strengthens leg muscles and improves coordination and balance. Child can also hold the stick for parent to hop over. Do this as many times as child likes.

4. Catch and Kick Child and parent stand seven to ten feet apart and toss a ball back and forth to each other (catching and tossing should both be done with two hands). At first, encourage child to toss the ball from under his body, between the legs, and eventually encourage the child (and demonstrate how) to toss/throw the ball from overhead. Also, practice kicking a ball back and forth and "trapping" (stopping) it with the foot. Start with you and your child only three or four feet apart, then move farther apart. Start with a big ball, and work down to a soccer ball.

5. Hula Hoop Stretch (seated) Child sits on floor with legs straight out in front but slightly separated, holding Hula Hoop (make sure posture is straight). Child then raises hoop overhead, stretching as high as possible (tell him to feel like someone is lifting up on the top part of the hoop), then slowly brings the hoop down to the floor, and stretching forward (back straight—never rounded), pushes the hoop out as far forward as he can (tell him to feel as if someone were pulling on the outer rim of the hoop). This is a wonderful stretch for the lower back, shoulders, and arms. It also teaches the child about keeping good posture through a stretch and about direction (up and down, in and out). This should be done two or three times at first, working up to ten repetitions.

part III: three years to six years

three to four years

1. Bunny Hop Have child imitate you hopping like a bunny. At first, take little hops (like a baby bunny), then take big hops (like a jackrabbit). You can vary this by becoming a kangaroo, a frog, a horse jumping over fences, a fox jumping over stone walls, etc. You can eventually teach your child how to hop in four different directions, each time hopping back to the center.

2. Spin a Yarn Suspend a ball of yarn so that it hangs about waist-high to your child, and give your child a Ping-Pong paddle to swat it with. Show your child how the yarn ball spins after each hit. Encourage your child to hit it hard, then soft, then hard, and so on.

3. Stick Hang Parent holds a broomstick or hockey stick so that child can grasp it with both hands and hang, at first, and eventually pull himself up to do a chin-up. (It's best for the parent not to bend his back over, but to raise or lower his arms as necessary, or kneel if necessary.)

4. Solo Bouncy Ball Child bounces ball and runs to the other side of it to catch it, then bounces again and runs to the opposite side to catch it.

5. Solo Under Bouncy Ball Child bounces ball hard so that it goes as high in the air as possible, then runs *under* it, spins around and catches it from the other side. This is great for coordination, balance, sprinting, and catching skills.

6. Flamingo Parent and child stand facing each other, and each raises one leg up and stands only on one foot; eventually teach child to place sole of raised foot on inner thigh of other leg and try to stand that way as long as he can. Allow the child to do this in a doorway at first so he can grab on to something if he needs to steady himself, eventually moving out into an open room.

7. Up and Down Parent and child stand facing each other, and both squat down slowly and then stand up high on tiptoes. This should be done fairly slowly to get the full effect of the stretch and strengthening exercise.

8. Mimic Parent and child or children stand in a circle. One person gets to be the director, and others follow. The director acts out an obvious movement (one that can easily be imitated by this group) and the others mimic the movement. It can be sweeping arms outward to "hug the world," dancing around with excitement, hugging arms in and "shivering in the cold," spreading arms outward and running to "soar like an eagle or jetplane," and so on. The possibilities for this activity are endless, and this can be a good aerobic session if done for ten to fifteen minutes continuously.

four to five years

NOTE: Do plenty of swinging, climbing, skipping, and hopping in your play periods. The more play exercises and games that improve balance, coordination, and agility, the better. Quiet times are good for encouraging hand and finger skills with writing and drawing, clay modeling, cutting and pasting, building block structures, etc.

1. Walk the Plank You and your child walk down a two-by-four board that's lying on the ground or floor in a variety of new ways: sideways, backward, eyes closed, etc. You can pretend you are surfing on a surfboard, walking the plank on a pirate ship, getting ready to dive off the high dive, and so on.

2. Toss and Turn Child tosses a tennis ball to the parent, then immediately spins around and waits to catch the ball as it's tossed back. Parent does the same thing. This refines skill of tossing a small sphere to a large target with one hand and catching it with two, and it also trains for balance.

3. Push-Off Child lies flat on floor, face down, then raises body up off floor with hands and feet, eventually balancing on palms of hands and tips of toes, buttocks pointed up in the air. This exercise works the muscles of the arms and shoulders, and is a good stretch for hamstrings, calves, and feet.

4. Through the Hoop Child stands holding Hula Hoop in front of him, then crawls through the hoop, letting it fall behind him. Then he does the same thing going back the other way. Encourage child to move his body through the hoop without touching his body to the hoop. You will want to spot your child at first doing this.

5. Box Stop Parent and child take turns stepping up onto a box, standing there, or spinning in a circle on the box, and stepping back down. There are many possibilities using the box, which should be about four or five inches high, and both parent and child can have their own box (you've seen step aerobics, no doubt—try some of those activities with your box).

6. Kickball You and your child kick a ball back and forth between you while walking in the same direction, ten to fifteen feet apart. One person kicks the ball, the other traps it and kicks it back. Now try it at a trot.

7. Laundry-Basketball Give the child a ball the size of a volleyball and first ask him to carry the ball and drop it into a laundry basket, then ask him to toss it in from a foot or two away, eventually moving farther and farther away until the child is able to toss from about five or six feet back and make a basket at least once in five tries.

1. Leapfrog Set up a goal line about thirty yards away from where your child and his partner are standing. Now he and his partner take turns leapfrogging each other out to the goal and back.

2. Back to Back Have your child stand back to back with a partner and hook their arms together. One of them calls out a movement (running forward or backward together, leg kicks, side hops, etc.) and they do five of them. Then the other partner calls out a different movement and they do five of those. They should keep taking turns calling out different movements and see how many movements they can come up with.

3. Tag There are all kinds of tag games, and they can be adapted to any size playing field and played with anywhere from two to twenty boys and girls. Someone is "It" until that person chases down and tags another person, who then becomes "It" until he tags someone else. "Rainy-day tag" can be played in a big open room by crawling or hopping on one foot instead of running. In "Nerf Ball Tag," the "It" person has to throw the ball and hit another person with it for that person to become "It."

4. One-on-One Nerf Baseball One child bats (using a foam ball and a big plastic bat or tennis racquet), and after a hit, tries to make it to a single base and back for a home run before the other player, the pitcher, can "tag" the batter out by touching him with the ball. After three outs, batter and pitcher change places. Kickball with a beach ball can be played the same way.

5. Three-Way Softball Throw Three children position themselves roughly in a triangle position about twenty to thirty feet away from one another while jogging. The child with the softball can throw only to someone who is in motion, which provides him practice in throwing to a moving target and provides the child catching with practice in getting to the ball, and stopping and positioning himself to catch the ball. Each player should touch the ball on every third throw, so that everyone gets equal practice with throwing and catching.

6. Toe Stands With his hands on his hips, the child stands up on his tiptoes for five to fifteen seconds. Then he does it with arms out to the sides, then with arms held straight over his head. Now he tries all three of those toe stands again, this time with his eyes closed, and tries to hold each one for five to fifteen seconds without losing his balance.

7. Tire and Plank Walk (for balance, balance stabilization, eye-foot coordination, multilimb coordination) Get four eight-foot two-by-four boards and four old tires and lay them out in your yard in a pattern like this:

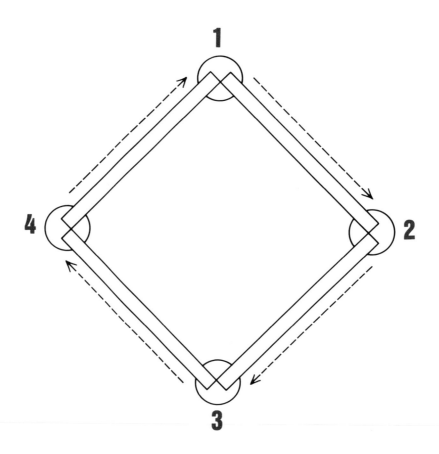

Now have your child walk the planks from position one to two, two to three, three to four, and back to one again. After she can do that three times without a foot touching the ground, have her try it by going from one to four to three to two and back to one. Try both routes sideways, on tiptoes, backward.

8. Soccer Ball Dribbling Kids can practice dribbling a soccer ball (kicking it from foot to foot), standing still at first, then at a walk, and finally at a slow run.

9. Agility Runs Set up milk containers or old tires or chairs, or whatever, in the pattern shown in the illustration. Kids can run, hop, or skip through this course, or have races through it (pretend it is a ski slalom course). You can also reverse the directions of the course and make it any size you want.

start

when arnold
was young

When I was twelve, I started spending a lot of time at the lake. The lake was very popular, and people from Graz would come to swim and lie in the sand. Since my father had taught me to swim when I was six, I was allowed to go to the lake by myself. My friends and I had swimming races and would chase each other along the shore like playful otters. We also had great mud fights. The bottom of the lake in the shallows was thick mud, and we would dive under and come up with handfuls of black ooze and make them into mudballs. Then we'd chase each other and throw the mudballs until we were completely covered.

It was at the lake that I first became involved in bodybuilding. There were older boys at the lake who were very big and strong. They worked out with weights and did exercises all the time. I remember staring at them and thinking how wonderful it must be to have a body like theirs.

They were also wonderful athletes who were very good at sports like swimming and wrestling and throwing the shot put. Everyone admired their skills and the way they looked, and when they worked out, a crowd gathered to watch. I knew I wanted to be like them, so I asked them to teach me. At first it was very hard and I couldn't even do chin-ups because my fingers were too weak. But I didn't give up. Just like when I made up my mind to carry more pails of water, more armloads of wood, and to kick the soccer ball farther than my friends, I made up my mind to do more chin-ups than anyone else at the lake. And I did. Then I knew I could accomplish whatever I wanted.

biBLiOGraPhY

The following is a list of works consulted in the research of these books:

COOPER, KENNETH H., M.D. *Kid Fitness: A Complete Shape-Up Program from Birth Through High School.* New York: Bantam, 1991.

AMERICAN ACADEMY OF PEDIATRICS. *Caring for Your Baby and Child, Birth to Age 5.* Edited by STEVEN P. SHELOV, M.D., F.A.A.P. (editor-in-chief), and ROBERT E. HANNEMANN, M.D., F.A.A.P. (associate medical editor). New York: Bantam, 1991.

ANDERSON, BOB. *Stretching.* Bolinas, Calif.: Shelter Publications, Inc., 1980.

ARNOT, ROBERT, M.D., and CHARLES GAINES. *Sports Talent.* New York: Viking Penguin, 1984.

EISENBERG, ARLENE, HEIDI E. MURKOFF, and SANDEE E. HATHAWAY, B.S.N. *What to Expect the First Year.* New York: Workman, 1989.

FIRKALY, SUSAN TATE. *Into the Mouths of Babes.* White Hall, Va.: Betterway Publications, Inc., 1984.

GAINES, CHARLES, and GEORGE BUTLER. *Staying Hard.* New York: Kenan Press, 1988.

GLOVER, BOB, and JACK SHEPHERD. *The Family Fitness Handbook.* New York: The Penguin Group, 1989.

KUNTZLEMAN, DR. CHARLES T. *Healthy Kids for Life.* New York: Simon and Schuster, 1988.

KUNTZLEMAN, CHARLES, and BETH and MICHAEL and GAIL MC-GLYNN. *Aerobics with Fun.* Reston, Va.: AAHPERD, 1991.

LEACH, PENELOPE, Ph.D. *Your Baby & Child from Birth to Age Five.* New York: Alfred A. Knopf, 1990.

McCOY, KATHY, and CHARLES WIBBELSMAN, M.D. *The New Teenage Body Book.* Los Angeles: The Body Press, 1987.

McINALLY, PAT. *Moms & Dads, Kids & Sports.* New York: Charles Scribners Sons, 1988.

MICHELI, LYLE J., M.D. *Sportswise: An Essential Guide for Young Athletes, Parents, and Coaches*. Boston: Houghton Mifflin, 1990.

ORLICK, TERRY. *The Cooperative Sports & Games Book*. New York: Pantheon Books, 1978.

PETRAY, DR. CLAYRE K., and SANDRA L. BLAZER. *Health-Related Physical Fitness: Concepts and Activities for Elementary School Children*. Edina, Minn.: Bellwether Press, 1987.

ROWLAND, THOMAS W. *Exercise and Children's Health*. Champaign, Ill.: Human Kinetics Books, 1990.

First and foremost, special thanks to Jane Forrestal Ellsworth. Thanks also to Stephen Lesko, graduate assistant at Springfield College, Springfield, Mass.; Dr. Mimi Murray, Springfield College; Donna Israel, nutrition expert at Cooper Institute; Janice M. O'Donnell, NHAHPERD; Diane Rappa, NHAHPERD; Tom Walton, physical education teacher at Rundlett Junior High School, Concord, N.H.; Professor Vern Seefeldt, Director, Youth Sports Institute, Michigan State University; Suzie Boos, RightStart Program, Children's Hospital of Illinois; Becky Davang, Kids' Aerobics, Sugar Land, Tex.; Susan Astor, President, Playorena, Roslyn Heights, N.Y.; Doug Moss, Marketing Specialist, Gymboree; Doug Curry, President (1991), MHAHPERD (Michigan); Sharon Nicosia, physical education teacher, Beaver Meadow Elementary School, Concord, N.H.; Beth Kirkpatrick, physical education teacher, Tilford Middle School, Vinton, Iowa, and past recipient of the Teacher of the Year Award from AAHPERD; Lani Graham, NASPE (part of AAHPERD); Lyle J. Micheli, M.D., Boston Children's Hospital; Dr. Charles T. Kuntzleman; Jill Werman; Louise McCormick, Plymouth State College, Plymouth, N.H.; President's Council on Physical Fitness and Sports, Washington, D.C.; American Alliance for Health, Physical Education, Recreation and Dance, Reston, Va.; Kenneth Cooper, M.D.; Dan Green; Charles L. Sterling, Ed.D.; Robert Arnot, M.D.; Judy Young, NASPE; Dave Camione, University of Connecticut, Storrs; Hal Jordan, Manchester YMCA, Manchester, N.H.; John Cates, University of California, San Diego; Jackie Aher, illustrator; Michael Palgon, Editor, Bantam Doubleday Dell; David Seybold; Jillian Neal, My Gym, Santa Monica, Calif.; Betty Glass, Santa Monica Alternative Schoolhouse, Santa Monica, Calif.